Praise f...
Can I Get a Do Over?

"Rick's energy and dynamic personality are evident in everything he does. He's always looking to reinvent himself, and is focused on taking his life to the next level. I wanna read this book!"

—**Tony Robbins**, *New York Times* bestselling author

"My life has always been about reinventing myself. From 22 years in the military, 17 years as a talk show host, 15 years as an author, and 30 years as a philanthropist, I have been in a constant state of 'do over.' I wish I had Rick's book; it would have made the entire journey easier."

—**Montel Williams**, philanthropist, bestselling author

"There's a recipe for inspiration, and it's in this book, y'all!"

—**Paula Deen**, cook, restaurateur, author, actress, and
Emmy Award–winning television personality

"Are you ready to take your life to the next level? *Can I Get a Do Over?* will inspire you to believe in your innate greatness and live the life of your dreams."

—**Dr. James Rouse**, naturopathic physician,
author of the Health Solutions series, and
founder of Optimum Wellness Media

"I think we, as responsible adults, should at some point in time take a breath and revaluate our lives and determine whether the path we took is the healthiest path in mind, body, and spirit. It is never too late to realize what beckons could be your passion; follow it for it will lead you to happiness. *Can I Get a Do Over?* is filled to the brim with passion."

—**Robert Caltabiano,** IFBB professional body builder, owner of Robert's One On One personal training

"The passion and energy that you see when Rick is on television is real and genuine; so are the inspiring stories of the people in his book. This is a great life lesson for any business or person to 'recreate' for a new chance at success and happiness."

—**James P. Jensen,** chairman of the board, New Ulm Telecom, Inc.

"In the fifteen years that I have known Rick, he never gives up, he always finds a way. I don't know if he was born with it or learned it from necessity, but his book is a living example of what you can do with a 'do over.'"

—**Lisa Roberston,** television personality and host of *PM Style*

"We learned the 'do over' at recess but never in the classroom. This book offers 'real life' lessons on one of the most important subjects for successful living in the 21st century."

—**Dan Wheeler,** television personality and author of *Best Seat in the House*

Can I Get a
DO OVER?

Unforgettable Stories of Second Chances and Life Makeovers

Rick Domeier
with Max Davis

Health Communications, Inc.
Deerfield Beach, Florida

www.hcibooks.com

Library of Congress Cataloging-in-Publication Data

Domeier, Rick
    Can I get a do over? : unforgettable stories of second chances and life makeovers /
[compiled by] Rick Domeier with Max Davis.
        p.   cm.
    Includes bibliographical references and index.
    ISBN-13: 978-0-7573-1563-3
    ISBN-10: 0-7573-1563-1
        1. Self-actualization (Psychology)—Anecdotes.   2. Self-realization—Anecdotes.
    3. Conduct of life—Anecdotes.   4. Biography—United States—Anecdotes.
    I. Domeier, Rick.   II. Davis, Max, 1960–
    BF637.S4C3437 2011
    155.2'4—dc22

                                                                    2010043026

Publisher: Health Communications, Inc.
            3201 S.W. 15th Street
            Deerfield Beach, FL 33442–8190

Cover photo courtesy of QVC
Cover design by Larissa Hise Henoch
Interior design and formatting by Lawna Patterson Oldfield

For Amy, Nick, and Josh . . .
and for Mom, Dad, and Jeanne,
You have given me so much.
With love,
I dedicate this book to you.

Contents

Foreword

Rick Domeier has written a book? That's hysterical! I didn't even know the man could read. Jokes aside, I've had the pleasure of working with Rick for more than fifteen years, and I love him! His energy and outlook on life are truly contagious (unlike the last man I dated—the only thing contagious about him was herpes, but that's another book).

Rick and I have done hours of live TV together, presenting my products on QVC. He's also contributed to many hilarious promo spots, and he starred with me in a soap opera spoof called "Stormy Rivers." He was so good, it should have been on network television.

Rick is an incredible host. Smart, full of energy, beyond quick on his feet, an amazing raconteur, and always in control of whatever situation comes his way. When he told me about writing a book on "do overs," I told him I thought it was a phenomenal idea.

If more people tried to "do over" their lives, I think the world would be a far better place. Personally, my life has had more do overs than Brad and Angelina have children. My first do over came early in my career when I dreamed of becoming a serious actress. After seven long years of knocking on doors that refused to open, sleazy agents who wanted no part of me, and finding out I had a mustache immune to Nair, I decided on my first do over. I changed horses and I began to concentrate on a gift that I'd always taken for granted: comedy.

Eventually I was booked on the *Tonight Show,* and Johnny Carson said, right on the air, "You're going to be a star." At that very moment I realized my do over from serious actress to comedienne actually had worked.

And lucky for me, it's still working. But, as I (and Rick) have learned, every time things start to go wrong, I'm not afraid to stop, evaluate, and call for, indeed, another do over. In fact, the only thing Rick feels has been reinvented more times than me is the wheel.

And now, at the age of 105 (give or take a decade), I'm an excellent example of what Rick's book preaches: Never let *anyone* say, "You can't do that," or "It won't work," or "You're finished" (except, of course, when they're talking about my sex life).

So, if you think you're a bit stuck in your life, do what Rick Domeier suggests and give yourself a do over. After reading his book, I think you'll agree with me that it's never, ever, *ever* too late! Good luck!

—*Joan Rivers*

Acknowledgments

To anyone who dares utter the phrase *You know, I think I wanna write a book!* please heed this warning: Do not attempt this endeavor alone. One lesson I've learned since embarking on this incredible journey many months ago: books are a team sport. Finding great people to play on that team is priority number one. With deep humility and endless gratitude, here are a few of the people who gave their precious time, opened their hearts, and let their creative juices flow in order to make this dream a reality.

Thanks to my amazing family, Amy, Nick, and Josh, for your love and support. Thanks for understanding when Daddy locked himself in his office to go do his "other job." You are a never-ending source of inspiration. Special thanks go to the herculean efforts of my coauthor, Max Davis. From creating compelling proposals to the zillions of late-night phone calls and early morning emails during the process to his "Let's keep it goin' and don't give up!" attitude and work ethic, I couldn't have asked for a better partner. To Carol Rosenberg, our kind and caring editor, as well as the entire team at HCI Books: Michele Matrisciani, Larissa Hise Henoch, Nicole Haye, Kim Weiss, Kelly Maragni, Lori Golden, and of course, Publisher Peter Vegso, who was crazy enough to let me "pitch" him the idea for the book in person. Thanks to my publicist Lisa Dubbels for such dedication and hard work while still remaining "Minnesota nice." Thanks to my agent, David Hale Smith, for taking a chance on Mr. Never-Been-Published and for sticking with me. Thanks to our web designer, Kristen Jacobs; and our trailer creator, Corey Yatkus. Thanks to the 24–7 "reinvention universe" that is QVC, and the myriad of amazing, proactive people that make it work. Thanks to the vast viewing audience of QVC. We've laughed a lot over the years. What I thought would be a sixth-month gig has turned out to be a sixteen-year career. Thank you for that. And lastly, to the remarkable people profiled in this book. It's a bit of an understatement to say that we couldn't have done this book without you. While each and every one you are extraordinarily unique, you had something in common: you were generous enough to share very personal, sometimes painful aspects of your lives. And each of you had a desire to make a difference, both in your lives and in the lives of other people. Your generosity of spirit will not be forgotten.

A pessimist sees the difficulty
in every opportunity;
an optimist sees the opportunity
in every difficulty.

—Sir Winston Churchill

Introduction

It was a hot, humid day in August, *and the sun was beating down on our driveway. The neighborhood basketball game was tied. My two sons, Nick and Josh, were on opposite teams, their competitive spirit alive and well. Elbows were flying and bodies were being shoved. It was getting intense, especially for me, the sweating, frazzled dad trying to referee. Was this a basketball game or a wrestling match? A quick pass, a missed shot, more elbowing and shoving for the rebound and . . .*

Bam! Smack!

"Ouch! Hey, no fair!"

"Dad, he hit me in the face! That's a foul!"

"No way! I was going for the ball!"

"What's the call, Dad?"

Too much mayhem. Ref didn't see it. Silence. Thinking.

"Dad?"

. . . More silence from a very confused referee.

Finally, in a burst of true brilliance, my son Nick spoke up: "Can I get a do over?"

◆ ◆ ◆ ◆

As a kid growing up in Minnesota, I remember games like that. Whether it was backyard softball, freeze tag, or kick the can (remember kick the can?!), inevitably there was a moment when someone would yell out, "Hey, can I get a do over?!" At that point, the game stopped, a conference was held, and cases were pleaded. Finally, someone (usually my friend Walt, the oldest, biggest kid) would say, "Okay, do over."

For that brief period in time the slate was wiped clean, the past forgotten, and permission was granted to try again. With newfound confidence and resilience, we jumped back into the game, more determined than ever to give it our best shot.

We were like that as kids—resilient, confident, and determined. We weren't afraid to "go for it" again. As time passed, however, we progressed from board games like Monopoly and LIFE (with make-believe money, plastic people, and pretend consequences), to the real game of LIFE (with *real* money, *real* people—okay, a few plastic people as well—and very *real* consequences).

Do we need to do an in-depth analysis of the various challenges we have faced over the last few years? I don't think so. Financial setbacks, the declining economy, job layoffs, record numbers of home foreclosures, strained relationships, too little sleep, stress, divorce, and oh, yeah, obesity. As my dad's favorite comedian Henny Youngman used to say, "And that's the *good* news!" Let's face it. It's depressing. Just watching CNN can make you want to crawl back into bed and *roll over* instead of *do over*.

I've always considered myself a positive person. I was blessed with extraordinary parents who grew up during the Great Depression. My late father fought for our freedom in World War II. So his old-school phrases like "enjoy the little things in life" and "see the glass as half full" were instilled at a very young age. The real problem is that, for many, the glass isn't half full, it's empty. Over time, the challenges I was seeing and reading about were no longer just news stories. They started to hit home with close friends and family members.

My wife, Amy, and I were discussing our future one night and asking ourselves what we'd do "if and when" the storm hit? I guess I'd have to reinvent myself," I said. Exactly how I would do this wasn't clear. I found myself studying people who had "reinvented their lives." As I read news articles and did research online, it became somewhat of an obsession for me. As Dr. Wayne Dyer mentioned to me one evening, "When you change the way you look at things, the things you look at change." I found that some of the most remarkable people were right in front of me or standing right next to me on air at QVC. That proactive "pick yourself up and get back in the game" spirit became a rallying call. It also became the inspiration for this book.

The stories within the pages and creases of *Can I Get a Do Over?* are about real people with real challenges. Most are told in their own words. That desire and drive to give ourselves a second chance is woven into the very fabric of our country. The

United States itself was founded on a do over. To celebrate this, we've also included several classic do-over stories from the past that shed light on our world today. My talented (and extraordinarily hardworking) coauthor, Max Davis, and I are on a mission: to inspire others with living, breathing examples of ordinary Americans who have made extraordinary, unforgettable changes in their lives.

What was most gratifying about setting out on this journey was *how inspired we became* ourselves. Getting to know the people in this book was a humbling, life-altering experience. The challenges and choices were as varied as their definition of "rock bottom." For some, it was simply a creative need, a calling. For some it happened because of circumstances thrust upon them and choices that had to be made in order for them to either sink or swim. For others, it was truly do over . . . or die.

Despite our particular situations and circumstances, regardless of our disappointments, hindrances, and failures, what if we *could* get a do over? Whether it involves our careers, dreams, relationships, or our physical bodies, the way we respond to the above question speaks volumes about who we are and about how we'll be spending the next five, ten, even twenty years of our lives. The good news is, the people you're about to meet have an answer to the question, "Can I get a do over?" It's a resounding "Yes!" Some stories will make you smile, some will make you put down that cookie and head to the gym, while others may make you want to immediately stop what you're doing and change directions, perhaps even start a new career. They'll make you question what's most important in your life. And all of them will remind you that, although our time on earth is oh-so limited, there is still time for a second chance. So go ahead, flip the page, enjoy the read, and give yourself permission to start again.

—Rick

The Great Holtzie

◆

Adam Holtz—The Greatest Thing to Happen to Kids Since Cake

"Twenty years from now you will be
more disappointed by the things you didn't do
than by the ones you did. So throw off the bowlines,
sail away from the safe harbor, catch the trade winds
in your sails. Explore. Dream. Discover."

—Mark Twain

I grew up in Margate, New Jersey, a little town along the coast. I was an average Jewish kid with an above-average sense of humor. When I was about seven years old, I started buying comedy albums from funny guys like Steve Martin and Robin Williams, and listened to them over and over again. After a few months of running around with a toy arrow through my head, I realized I too had a gift for making people laugh.

Life was pretty easy until the sixth grade, when I began struggling in school. That was back before they diagnosed kids with

1

ADHD, so I was just called "smart but lazy" or unfocused. My formal diagnosis of ADHD didn't come until about twenty years later, but by then it simply confirmed what everyone already knew. Throughout middle school and high school, I had always felt like I was smart, but I could never understand why classes were so difficult. This sense that I was intelligent but somehow couldn't get my act together led to a lot of embarrassment. I became good at covering up my perceived shortcomings with humor. I have always been quick-witted, and making people laugh felt good.

When it came time to go to college, I had bad grades but good SAT scores, thanks to several SAT courses I had taken. This is a perfect example of how I learned how to maximize my strengths and mitigate my weaknesses. I often found it very difficult to concentrate during long school days, but I could hyperfocus during the shorter SAT classes and learn strategies for test taking. I could really shine when it came to tasks that provided instant gratification. As a result, I got into several colleges. Harvard wasn't interested, but I suddenly had options.

I eventually made it through college, struggling like I did in high school. I had my degree, but no idea what I wanted to do with it. I had majored in marketing and communications with a vague plan of working in advertising, but I could not get interested enough in the field to pursue it. So I went through a bunch of crappy jobs before settling as a recruiting executive. I loved it at first. It was the late nineties and the IT industry was booming. Loads of money, countless happy hours, and single life in a big city. What more could I want? Well . . . I wanted a lot more, but I still didn't know what "it" was. Ironically, I spent all day helping other people land their dream jobs while my own career and life felt so unfulfilling.

For ten years, I worked as a recruiter. In the back of my mind, there was always this dilemma of "Is this it?" or "What will my legacy be in this world?" I'd look at some of my older coworkers and think, *Do I want to be that guy whose greatest joy during the day seems to be a smoke break?* I wanted to do something creative, but I also wanted to eat and pay rent. Finding something I was passionate about that still allowed me to pay my bills seemed impossible.

Meanwhile, my sister had her sons. It didn't take me long to realize that they loved me, and so did almost every other kid I met. Over the years, I started to realize that I kind of liked them too. I never felt intimidated or overwhelmed when I babysat my nephews. I simply enjoyed our time together. When they acted up, I was always able to maintain control, and I never lost my cool. And, much to my surprise, if I was funny to adults, I was a comic genius to kids. The time I spent with my nephews felt satisfying and rewarding. I respected them and took my responsibility as a caregiver and mentor very seriously while still having fun. I used to think to myself, *If money didn't matter and I could start over, I would become a kindergarten teacher.* That seemed like the dream job for me. But I didn't want to go back to school, so I stuck with recruiting.

Then, in March 2007, my girlfriend, Sandra, her daughter,

Ava, and I went to Washington, D.C., to visit some friends who had two children. While the adults were doing their thing, I was entertaining the three kids. I was doing some lame shtick that had the kids in stitches. When my friend Beth observed how the kids were responding, she said, "Oh my gosh, Adam, you should be like a children's entertainer or something!" At that moment a light in my head clicked on. I knew instinctively that this was what I was supposed to do. I wanted to make kids laugh! I was about to become the world's greatest (and only) stand-up comedian for kids!

When stepping out of the traditional box of security and risking a dream, it's critical to have someone in your corner cheering you on. Sandra was that person. (She is now my wife, and we have added to our family with a beautiful daughter named Claire. But that will be covered in the movie about my life.) She knew how funny I was and she regularly witnessed my unique ability to relate to kids. She saw how Ava had taken to me at a time when a boyfriend could have been roadblocked with flat-out rejection. Sandra was the ultimate partner for this because she totally bought into it without ever questioning me, and she often got excited about my ideas. It can be boiled down to four words, "She believes in me." Kenny Rogers was so right!

At this point, my second greatest asset next to Sandra was . . . wait . . . my third greatest asset next to Sandra and my comedic brilliance was my ADHD. My old buddy was back, and this time he wasn't going to screw everything up! ADHD has a way of making people leap before they look, and that was just what my new career needed. This moment at the crossroads didn't call for thoughtfulness, introspection, and convention. It required a voice yelling in my ear, "LET'S GET IT ON, JOKE BOY!" My ADHD provided that push. I dove in headfirst and never looked back.

Let me take a few moments to point out a couple things. First, I didn't have an act, but I wasn't going to let a minor detail like that stop me. I had something far more valuable. I had a killer idea that was original and marketable. The other thing you need to know about was my crippling stage fright. The first and only time I was onstage was during my bar mitzvah, but I can't really remember anything about it because I was so terrified. I do remember my parents gave me a VCR, which was pretty cool for a thirteen-year-old in 1983. That thirty-pound top-loading beauty was pretty sweet. All joking aside, I knew I couldn't let lack of experience and fear stop me. I knew in my core that I had the ability to pull this off. Plus, I had spent my entire adult life looking for something that I felt passionate about and I had finally found it. Nothing could get in my way!

I was glad that I had actually paid attention in some of my marketing classes. My shtick needed a shtick. I understood the importance of branding, and I was very clear on what I wanted my brand to be. Funny, relatable, hip, and edgy. Costumes were a nonstarter. I didn't want to wear some creepy clown getup or a stupid vest with a bunch of chili peppers on it that screamed, "I'm ZANY!" My anti-costume stance went against advice I was getting at the time. One guy actually suggested I wear overalls and a farmer's hat. It seems like there is an unwritten law that says, "To make kids laugh you must dress like a schmuck." Nope! I wasn't going to do that. Kids think their dads are funny. I was going to dress like a dad. But not one of those dads who wears pleated Dockers and a Club Room polo. I was more of a Fred Perry and jeans kind of guy. Whatever . . . I'm hip! This also allowed me to be more relatable to the parents. I am, and was, my customer. Do you know any clowns who can say that?

Next, I came up with the name "The Great Holtzie." My last name is Holtz. For most of my life, I had been called Holtzie by friends. (Obviously I went to school with guys who weren't known for their nickname skills.) Looking back, I might have picked a different name if I had thought about it for more than three seconds. "The Great Holtzie" sounds like a 1920s magician with a curly moustache or the name of a character from one of my sister's Judy Blume books. However, all of that debate is moot now because my ADHD impulse left me with about five seconds between coming up with the name and registering the Internet domain.

With my name and my eternal place in cyberspace taken care of, I contacted my friend Laurie to help me with my website. She is a fantastic graphic designer. There seems to be another children's entertainer rule that states, "All websites must be L-A-M-E." I told her that I wanted my website to look classy and clean, without visual clutter. I needed an aesthetic that appealed to a mother's eye. I knew that my online presence was critical to my success. Since I didn't have an act yet, I obviously didn't have a reputation, a following, or an income . . . you get the picture. My website was the key to conning the world into believing I was the "greatest thing to happen to kids since cake." (I came up with that line.)

So with my website under construction and my business cards ordered, it was time to start the fourth day of my new career. It's true! I came up with the idea on a Saturday. On Sunday, I mulled everything over, and on Monday and Tuesday, I accomplished everything I just described.

Now it was time to mold reality. I started by posting press releases on a couple of the free press release sites. I wrote an article about making a birthday party successful. I'd never done a birthday party before, but I had an idea of how they would work. I just needed to get my name out there and create Internet search results. I did this for about a week. During the same time I started to write my routine. I also infiltrated a couple of mom's Yahoo Groups and other message boards. Nobody could recommend me yet, but they were starting to get familiar with my name. I also built a list of toy and clothing stores so I could start networking.

Only three weeks passed before I performed my first gig. It was for my friend's child's birthday party. I said, "Dude, you've got to let me do a show." My friend agreed, but he told me that under no conditions would he be paying me. I said, "Fine" and asked if I had to pay him. Thankfully, no money exchanged hands that day. I was more excited than nervous and more funny than not. The kids loved me and the parents were taken by my fresh approach. I was a hit! As I drove away from the party, I had such a fulfilled and satisfied feeling.

Since that day, there's never, ever been any doubt in my mind that I made the right decision. Here's another interesting thing: before I did my career do over, I regularly suffered from dreams rooted in stress and anxiety. When I became The Great Holtzie, those dreams stopped. Never again will I wake up thinking that I missed a test!

One week after I did the party for my friend, I landed my first paying show from an ad I placed on Craigslist. I was developing an act that was for kids, but it was also something that the parents could enjoy. In just a few weeks, I had written a forty-minute act that, in theory, was going to make parents laugh along with their kids. When it came time to perform my first official show, things actually went better than I'd imagined. They loved it! The kids *and* the parents! Everything was just great! It was a surreal moment when the mother handed me a check. For someone who had never done this before, who had never performed in front of people, who was afraid to speak in front of an audience, I felt that I had found my gift and was doing what I was born to do. For the first time in my life, I had a path that I created. I had a plan that I hatched. I finally had the beginnings of a legacy that I could someday be proud of.

I got my act listed on Nickelodeon's website, gocitykids.com. After each show, I asked my customers to write little reviews on the site. I was proactive about using every little success to leverage it for another win. While I still love doing small shows, like birthday parties and camps, I have done hundreds of shows for larger and larger audiences, including playing to packed houses at theaters and comedy clubs in the Philadelphia area.

Because I offer something unique, reporters love my story. I have been featured in many local magazines and newspapers. I have also won a bunch of awards and have been asked to speak about my career at the local Rotary Club. Philadelphia's PBS station, WHYY, even did a feature story on me for their monthly arts program. This has all happened in fewer than three years.

So far, my career has been filled with nothing but highs. First and foremost, making kids laugh rocks! That is why I do what I do. Beyond that, the personal satisfaction of finding something that was my calling has provided me with an inner peace that I'll probably take to my deathbed. Before I took the risk of reinventing my life, I lived in confusion, always mentally wondering and wandering. It got to the point when I was getting closer to forty, I asked myself, "What's my legacy?" I really cared about that, and I cared about trying to give something back to the world.

That desire has led me to donate a lot of shows to charities and perform at children's hospitals. Those shows are great. Because I am dealing with sick children, I work extra hard to treat them exactly like healthy kids. I even tease them a bit, which is exactly the opposite of how most adults act toward ill children. At the first hospital show, the kids clearly loved it, but I wondered if I had gone too far and was too edgy for some of the parents. But then a dad told me, "You're like a Pixar movie. It's funny for adults and kids." More important, a mom told me it was the first time she had seen her daughter laugh in a long time.

I think back to some of those things that made me laugh when I was eight or nine years old and I realize they were the highlights of my childhood. I hope someday I am a childhood memory. It would be cool if forty years from now someone said, "Remember that bald guy who came to our school and made burp jokes?" That would be pretty satisfying, at least for me.

Adam Holtz continues to dazzle his audiences. He won the Best of Philly Award in 2008, the My Fox Philly Best Entertainment Award, Best Party Entertainer in Philadelphia, and Nickelodeon's Parents' Pick Award. To watch Adam in action, visit his website www.thegreatholtzie.com.

Taking Life by Storm

◆

René Uzé—Owner of
Forum Salon in Baton Rouge, LA

"Tough times never last, but tough people do."

—Robert H. Schuller

Cutting hair has been in my blood since my junior year of high school in 1977. I got hooked from watching the work of a family friend who had a haircutting business. The summer before my senior year, I started cutting hair right out of my bedroom. I got an old shower curtain and put it on the floor, swiped one of our kitchen bar stools, and hung up an old 1940s-circa mirror that my dad had given me. It was a pretty rough setup, but I was in business. I played baseball that summer and my buddies on the team started coming to me for haircuts. Then they started bringing their girlfriends. A couple guys even brought their moms. It was nuts. From that summer throughout my entire senior year, I booked three people five days a week and was getting three dollars a haircut. Finally, after much contemplation and some

11

encouragement from my brother, I raised my price to a whopping five dollars! I was really rolling in the dough!

The work never slowed down. I got busier and busier, and the more I thought about it, I said to myself, "Hey, René, this is a pretty nice setup you got here. You're warm in the winter, cool in the summer, and you have all these ladies coming, which is a pretty good perk." And it was a creative outlet for me as well.

After high school, I continued to cut hair out of my bedroom and build my clientele, even though I was also enrolled in cosmetology school. Then, shortly before I graduated, a woman who owned a modeling agency came in looking for a male haircutter. I was recommended and she hired me on the spot. I began working at her salon five days a week cutting hair for all her models. What a dream! I also learned how to do makeup and things like that. We did fashion shows. I taught makeup and hair care. It was wild and fun, it got my name out there, and I was able to keep my old clientele. One thing led to another until I eventually had my own shop. I soon had ten stylists working for me six days a week, and was open from 8:00 AM to 9:00 PM, Monday through Saturday. By 2005, before Hurricane Katrina hit, it was one of the top high-end shops in the New Orleans area. In addition to doing hair, we did manicures, pedicures, and massages. We were really rocking.

My success in the hair business allowed me the opportunity to build my dream home, an authentic 1850s Cajun-style antebellum on thirty picturesque acres. It was like something right out of the movies—massive oak trees with moss, an orange grove of fifty trees, and sixty pecan trees. It was a paradise.

A day before Hurricane Katrina hit, my girlfriend and I evacuated to Baton Rouge about two hours north. Like everybody else, we thought we'd only be gone for a couple days. We bounced around from house to house in Baton Rouge staying with whoever could take us in. Then I received some photographs from a friend of mine in New Orleans. It took about a week for me to get the pictures or any solid news about our places because the phone systems were all down. They were taken from his boat, and I could barely see the roofs of the buildings. My shop, full of equipment, had sixteen feet of water in it. My dream home was flooded as well. When I saw the photos my heart sank and I knew in my gut that I would not be going back. Everything I had worked for my whole life was gone with the storm.

I said to my girlfriend, "Forget about it. It's over. We're moving on from here. We're not looking back. It's going to be a new beginning, and it's going to be greater than it ever was. I know we're going to miss everything, and I'm going to miss my home, the house, and the country, but this is it. It's over. We're moving on."

I wanted to cry and give in to despair, but I knew I couldn't do that. It would destroy me. I always believed that you can't change the past. You can only move forward. I'm not going to worry about what happened, and I'm not going to worry about what might happen. I'm going to live today, and if I wake up tomorrow and I'm breathing and I'm healthy, I'm going to get off of it and I'm gonna make something happen.

Just ten days after the storm hit, I was lying in bed thinking to myself, *René, man, you've gotta get to work. You can't lose all your clients!* As I was pondering the situation and thinking about what I needed to do, another idea hit me. Seemingly, my clients were all gone, but I knew if I was in Baton Rouge, so were a large percentage of them. I also knew most of them were not going back either. So, I came up with what I believed was an inspired idea. Desperation begets inspiration. I said to myself, *René, you've got to go to the Mall of Louisiana and get a job cutting hair because you know they'll be there.* I reasoned that if they lost everything like I did, they'd be there shopping for clothes. That was my idea, and that's exactly what I did. I didn't waste time grieving my losses. I couldn't afford to.

My girlfriend and I walked into the Mall of Louisiana for the first time. It's huge, one of the largest malls in the South. We walked around for six or seven hours trying to determine the entrance with the most volume coming in and out. When we did that, we noticed that this entrance just happened to have a chain hair salon near it. I told my girlfriend, "I'm going in there and getting a job." I knew I had to humble myself and do whatever it took.

"How do you know they'll hire you?"

"They have to."

So I walked in and said, "Let me talk to the manager."

She was a wonderful lady named Billy. "Let me tell you what's going on," I began. "I've been doing hair for twenty-five years and built a high-end, eight-chair salon from the ground up. I lost it all in Katrina. I'm here. I need a job. The only things I have left are my clients who are coming to this mall, and I can't lose them. Give me a week and I'll bring a lot of new business in here. I promise you that. If I don't, then you do what you have to do with me. But I'm going to make this thing happen for you and for me. I have to."

"Alright, when can you start?" was her reply.

"How about tomorrow morning?" I responded.

The next day, just two weeks after Hurricane Katrina wiped me out, I was working. I can't tell you how many times I walked in and out grabbing people I knew. I had some business cards made, and I just kept giving them to everybody. I'd give out five or ten cards and ask each person to hand them to everyone they knew. They did, and I got busy, busy, busy. Little did I know how inspired my plan that night really was. I worked at that salon until I got back on my feet and had built my clientele back up. Billy and I became great friends. She's a wonderful lady. I owe it to her. And hope I can give back to her one day. I'm sure I will.

During this time of rebuilding my life and business, the insurance informed me they were only going to cover one-fourth of what I'd lost. That was the second big blow. Then, as if that wasn't enough, one day while I was applying my roll-on deodorant, I found a lump under my left armpit. Long story short, the doctor took it out and ran a biopsy. The next week I found myself in the doctor's office sitting on the exam table. He solemnly informed me that it was cancer. It felt like someone had punched me in the gut and then kicked me. When the doctor was finished, I asked him to leave me alone for a few minutes and please turn off the lights when he went out. When he was gone, I lay back in that dark, cold room and said to myself—it seemed I'd been spending a lot of time talking to myself those days—I said, "Okay, René, here's the deal. There's not a chance in the world that this thing is going to kill you. You're not going to let it. There's no way after you've already lost so much. There's just no way. You're going to kick this thing in the ass! You're going to get up, and things are going to be better than ever."

I don't know what made me think that, but that's what I believed. The more I laid there thinking, the more I knew that I would beat it.

Later, they did a couple of extremely painful bone marrow extractions and determined that I had CLL, chronic lymphocytic leukemia. I started chemotherapy right away and it really kicked me and sapped my energy. Before the treatments I'd been planning on opening my new salon in Baton Rouge. I remember before my first treatment a relative said, "I just don't understand why you want to open a business, especially when you're sick."

"Hey, man. I'm not sick!" I told him. "I'm taking medication and getting treatment. Don't call me sick! And I'm opening my business. I have to or I'll die!"

"Okay," he said, "but I think you're crazy, man."

"I know. A lot of people do. But that's what's happening."

During my chemotherapy treatments, which were every three weeks for several months, I had my laptop with me and I was planning my shop, my PR, and my marketing materials. And, in June 2007, not quite two years after Hurricane Katrina, I opened Forum Salon with nine employees. As of today it's been three years and there are now fifteen of us, and Forum is one of the top high-end salons in Baton Rouge.

In the beginning of the chemotherapy treatments, the doctor said my leukemia was at 30 percent of my blood cells. That is the ratio of bad cells to the good cells. I asked him what he was expecting it to be after the treatments. He said, "You're young and strong—we hope to get it down to the 18 to 20 percent range."

"Only 18 to 20 percent?" I said. "I tell you what, doctor. I'm going for 0 to 6 percent. How's that?"

"Listen, I've been at this game for a long time, and the odds of that aren't likely."

"Hey, man, you expect what you want, but I'm going to expect what I want. I'm going for 0 to 6 percent, and I'm ready to get started."

At the end of my last treatment he walked in and was smiling bigger than I'd ever seen him smile.

"What's my number?" I asked.

"Two percent!"

"I told you!"

"You were right, René. You were right."

"Man, I can't give up. I have everything to lose, and that's why I keep this attitude."

We continued talking like pals, and I asked him, "What's the life expectancy now that I'm at 2 percent?"

"Seven years."

"Okay, I'll go at least twenty."

"René, I know you have a positive attitude, but the average life expectancy is seven years."

"You're making me mad, doc. Now I'm going for twenty-five!"

He looked at me like I was crazy.

"Okay, I'm done here," I said. "I'm going to MD Anderson Cancer Center."

"But why?"

"Because the way you see it, I'm in a seven-year fight for my life, and I know that's not true. MD Anderson is working on cures, and I want a second opinion."

"Well, if that's what you want," he said, looking annoyed. Then he rushed out of the office. I thought to myself, *Are you kidding me? This is my life we're dealing with. I'd do this for my dog. And you're getting all bent because I want a second opinion.*

So I went to MD Anderson and I talked with one of the top doctors there. He told me I had done well with the medicine and that I was in great shape. He ran some tests and said everything looked good.

"I'm here to volunteer for the test studies," I said. "I'm single. I have no children. I have very little family and I've lived a good life. If I help people through what happens to me, I'm good, and that's why I'm here."

"You're serious?" he asked.

"It's what I want."

"That's admirable, René, but I sit on the board that picks the patients we use for these studies and you wouldn't get picked."

"Why?"

"Because you're too healthy!"

"So what do I do now?"

"Go back to Baton Rouge and live a long, fulfilling life. René," he said, "you're not going to die from this. You have a better chance of dying in a car accident."

I laughed out loud.

"What's so funny?"

"I live in Baton Rouge and have a four-and-a-half-hour drive home!"

René Uzé is all about giving back. "Baton Rouge embraced me when Hurricane Katrina destroyed everything I had in the New Orleans area. It is the people of this fine community that I thank for the opportunity to reestablish my business, and now it is time for me to give back to others who have also experienced hardship or adversity in their lives." One of the ways René is giving back is by producing the television show *Makeover 225*. In each episode, one deserving individual is treated to a makeover and more by a caring and gracious group of Baton Rouge businesses and individuals who share René's same philosophy of giving back. Each recipient is provided with services to enhance their outer appearance as well as fulfilling a dream, wish, goal, or need they might have.

Do Over or Die

♦

George Stella—Bestselling Author, Chef, and Nutritional Expert

"We are our choices."

—Jean-Paul Sartre, 1905–1980

I was born in 1959, and even though we were relatively poor, I had a very happy childhood. One thing I learned early on is that happiness doesn't necessarily derive from money. I had three sisters, so there were four of us kids, and our mother always tried to make us feel special. She was the Martha Stewart of our small town in rural Connecticut, always canning the grapes that grew in the grove, growing vegetables, sewing this, and making that. I remember waking up many mornings to a house filled with wonderful aromas because my mother was already in the kitchen baking or cooking up something special. On a lot of those days, I knew that my cousins would be coming over and we would have a big meal then play games like canasta. It was a wonderful time of food and fun, and it greatly influenced me to become a chef.

Later, my family moved to South Florida, and at age fourteen, I took a job as a dishwasher at my best friend's uncle's restaurant. While there, his uncle taught me how to cook, and by fifteen, even though I was only in high school, I was a chef for a Mexican restaurant. School took a lot of my time, but because we were poor, I had to earn a living too. If I didn't want to wear my father's psychedelic 1960s straight pants to school, then I had to have a job so I could buy something different.

It was also when I was fifteen that my health problems began. One day after returning from a school trip, I got violently ill with acute pericarditis. That's where there's inflammation of the pericardium around the heart. It was so bad that they had to do a pericardiocentesis on the spot. While I was wide awake, with no anesthesia, they stuck a needle under my rib cage into my heart and drew a quart of fluid out because my heart was about to burst. It was the most painful thing I've ever experienced. My heart went into V-fib (ventricular fibrillation) and the monitor went crazy. I was watching the whole thing and almost squeezed the male nurse's hand to death. They had the paddles over me, but I came out of it and they didn't have to use them.

They put me on 120 milligrams of steroids a day to keep the inflammation down and to keep the fluids away from my heart. For a three-year period, even with all those medications, I still experienced recurrence after recurrence of the pericarditis. Finally, when I was nineteen, I was sent to the Cleveland Clinic in Cleveland, Ohio, to have a pericardiectomy through open-heart surgery. After the procedure, the pericardium would no longer hold fluids and that would be the end of the pericarditis, but it would also be very dangerous to live the rest of my life with no padding around my heart.

The day before my open-heart surgery I was called into the surgeon's office, and he told me, "You don't need open-heart surgery. Your whole problem is you're overmedicated. I'm referring you to a med specialist." When I saw the specialist, the first thing he said was "I'm surprised you're still alive."

I was taking massive doses of prednisone every day. Anytime I had the least bit of discomfort, the prescription was more steroids. Back then it was a new drug, and they didn't know that much about it. Today, we know you only give someone 5 milligrams to start and taper them off over a five-day period. I was on 120 milligrams a day for three and a half years! When they took me off, I went into drug withdrawal and my weight shot through the roof. I had the balloon face and everything. At nineteen, I was about 175 pounds. By twenty-five, I was 300 pounds.

The steroids had messed up my metabolism, but also I wasn't paying attention to my eating habits. At that point, I dropped out of college and totally focused on cooking. Good cooks were making pretty good money, and I knew how to cook, so I took it seriously. Soon, I met my wife, Rachel, had a child by the time I was twenty-one, and a few years later we had our second child. Driven to succeed, I became one of the top chefs in South Florida.

Because I was a cook, I was around food all day, but I wouldn't eat because I was so busy. After long, grueling days in the restaurant kitchen, I found myself getting home and eating whatever

I could to make up for that day of missed meals. I would be famished and would eat leftovers and snack foods and sugary processed desserts. It didn't matter what it was as long as I ate as much as I could, as quick as I could after that day of fasting. I had no understanding of eating to stay healthy and even eating to lose weight. What was worse is that because of *my* poor eating habits and the poor foods that we had in the house, my whole family was following my example, and together, the four of us weighed a half ton.

Then, at twenty-five, weighing 300 pounds, I had a heart attack. I was pushing, pushing, pushing to be successful in the restaurant business. In the morning, I would do the cooking for two restaurants. After that, I'd put a fresh shirt and tie on and be the manager for the afternoon at both places, going back and forth. I only slept when I got a chance. Even though I was in the hospital for two weeks, I was in a state of total denial. What should have been a wake-up call meant nothing because I felt great when I got out. As a result, I went straight back to work and to my old habits like nothing ever happened.

My success as a chef continued at the first California cuisine restaurant in South Florida, the first wood-burning grill, the first show kitchen. Today, the food that we were creating is known as "Floridian cuisine." Yes, I felt I was at the top of my field. But unfortunately, my family and I continued our unhealthy ways and continued to gain weight. It had gotten so bad that by age thirty-five I was 467 pounds, needed a wheelchair to get around, and was forced to give up the career I loved. We survived on

Social Security disability and by supplementing our income at flea markets.

My son, Christian, at age fifteen, was 306 pounds and my wife, Rachel, had gone from 135 pounds to 205 pounds. Anthony, my other son, was around 225 pounds but gaining. Because of their weight issues, the kids were having trouble in the public schools and we pulled them out to homeschool, which in the end worked out for the better.

I'm one of those guys who has to reach rock bottom before they change. You would think that seeing my family suffer, being in a wheelchair, and on Social Security would be rock bottom, but it wasn't. For the next year and a half I was in and out of the hospital with pneumonia, required the use of a breathing machine at home, and inhalers. Now and again I needed doses of steroids because the fluid was building back up in my system, and my heart just couldn't pump through the full length of my extra-large body.

The tragedy was, we were still eating all the wrong foods and I was the major perpetrator. I had no conception of what healthy foods were. Most chefs back then didn't. We were uneducated about nutrition because it wasn't an issue like it is today.

Rock bottom finally came when I was approved for Medicare instead of Medicaid. There's a big difference, you know. Medicaid is what you get when you're poor and on food stamps. Medicare is what you get when you're on Social Security. When I got my card, I immediately made an arrangement to go to a cardiologist because I was on several cardiac medicines. But when I got there they said, "I'm sorry, sir. We can't treat you."

"What do you mean you can't treat me?" I asked.

"You do have Medicare, but you can't use the card for two years. With Medicare there is a two-year holding period."

"That's ridiculous," I said. "If I'm sick enough to have a Medicare card that means I'm sick enough to die tomorrow. If you don't check my levels, I can't continue to take this medicine."

"I'm sorry. There's nothing we can do."

I called my congresswoman here in Orlando and she told me, "Join the club. They tacked on this provision designed to lessen the roles of Medicare recipients by making them wait two full years from the time deemed eligible and then you die —everybody dies."

After all those years and crises, it finally hit me, "George, if you don't take control of your life and lose weight, you're going to die." That was the difference. I mean, I was given an ultimatum. It was like a gun being put to my head. Then, I started thinking about my family, and it became about them, not just me. I realized I had to do something. Luckily, the answer came along at the same time.

Part of the answer came in the book *Dr. Atkins' New Diet Revolution*. I didn't really do the Atkins diet, but it gave me the raw motivation to finally start looking at what I was eating. The book inspired and motivated me to know I could be successful. Rachel read one paragraph to me out of the book, and she said, "It says here, George, you can eat all the bacon, eggs, steak, and cheese you want and you're going to lose weight."

"That's a diet for me," I said. We went off to an all-you-can-eat buffet. I took everything that contained bacon, eggs, steak, cheese, and lean protein. I had four platesful of steak, 100 steamers dipped in butter, and a dash of broccoli, because I knew that was low in carbohydrates. I went back to my seat and unbuttoned my sixty-eight-inch pants. On the way home we started laughing. "This is ridiculous," I said. "You can't lose weight eating like this." Two days later, I was down four pounds. That's how I started, and that's all I knew, until I dove into what carbohydrates were, the difference between good carbs and bad, what whole grains were, and other healthy food secrets. I took what I called "stereotypical" Atkins advice. I took the advice and expanded upon it, improved it. You have to have good carbohydrates, which is what I write about in my books. In eighteen months I was down 200 pounds and eventually down to my present weight of 205. That's a weight loss of 262 pounds! And it wasn't just me. My whole family followed suit. We had fun. It was the same type of fun that I told you about in the beginning when I'd wake up to my mom cooking and those wonderful family times. That was happening in our house every day. Christian was 305 pounds, and he lost 165 pounds down to 140. Anthony went from 240 down to 165, a loss of 75 pounds. Rachel went from 205 to 128, a loss of 77 pounds. Our whole family has lost a total of 579 pounds!

Obviously, we are all happier and healthier. Another thing was my son's friends also lost weight, and so did their parents. That was important because it told me we were on to something.

We were having fun. We were eating. We started on the Atkins diet, but we reinvented it and made it unique, which turned out to be a great help for other people as well. You can imagine how many people are caught up in this obesity epidemic. People are constantly coming up to us asking, "How'd you do it?" We knew we had to find a way to share this information.

We started locally by creating the Low Carb Home Chef Service where we did exactly for our clients what we did for ourselves. We would take the bad foods out of their homes, shop for them, and then refill their homes with good, healthy food. Then we'd give them support mechanisms. We created a DVD series that was eventually turned into a local TV show. Not long after that, it was picked up nationally. One thing led to another and the show got on the Food Network. The books followed, and now I travel around the country spreading the message. Rachel, the boys, and I feel blessed that we can somehow help others overcome the same struggles we overcame.

There are a whole lot of people in hopeless despair because of weight illness. They think it's too late, that they can't turn their situation around, but our family is proof positive that they can! You can! Regardless of how you feel, you are not past the point of no return. There's always a chance; there's always a way.

After his success living a low-carb lifestyle, George worked as a chef at Walt Disney World's Grand Floridian Resort hotel and in fine restaurants such as Victoria & Albert's and Citricos. With a success story such as the Stella family's it was not long before George and Rachel were featured in several magazine and newspaper stories, as well as on television on networks such as Fox, CNN, and CBS Television Nightly News in Orlando, Florida. They have also appeared regularly on Fox News Channel's national morning news show *Fox & Friends,* and ABC's *The View,* where they have demonstrated various low-carb dishes such as gourmet pizza, key lime cheesecake, and strawberry shortcake martinis.

Along with his weekly show *Low Carb and Lovin' It* on Food Network, George looks to share his and his family's success by preparing naturally low-carb foods and teaching viewers the benefits of a low-carb lifestyle. George has authored four books, including his bestselling *George Stella's Livin' Low Carb: Family Recipes Stella Style.*

Sing My Life

◆

Meghan Cary—
Award-Winning Singer/Actress

"When you play music you discover a part of
yourself that you never knew existed."

—Bill Evans

I was raised in Hershey, Pennsylvania, a small town of 12,000
where the streetlights are shaped like Kisses and it smells like
chocolate. As a kid I went to Hersheypark, a huge amusement
park similar to Disneyland, only it's snuggled in the hills of
Pennsylvania. This was where my friends and I usually hung out.
It was good, clean fun with a touch of magic.

Not only were the rides at the park great, but they had top-
notch theatrical shows that I loved to watch. When I saw the
singers and dancers onstage, I'd think, *This is so cool. I wish I
could do that.* I had this romantic dream of what it would be
like. I don't know where it came from, because no one in my
family was musical, and I really didn't play any instruments. On

the contrary, I was a total science geek and wound up going to Duke on an academic scholarship, majoring in premed.

During the summer between my freshman and sophomore years, I got a job at Hersheypark as a stage manager. When the singers and dancers would perform, I can remember thinking, *They're actually getting paid to sing and dance. Wow. How cool is that!* The cast members had parties on their off time and because I worked there, I got to go. At that time, I had learned three chords on the guitar because I was really drawn to it. I tried to play, but it was a struggle. I just didn't really know how. I hadn't had any formal lessons and was trying to teach myself. So I focused on singing. And, because I was around singers that sang country, I started singing country songs. I was always singing and people even started joking about it. After a while they were coming up to me and saying, "You should audition for the Hoedown." That was the country music show at the park. So, the next summer I auditioned and got cast.

They sent us to New York for a week of studio rehearsals, and then we came back to Hersheypark for a week of rehearsals there. The show was great, and I loved it. In fact, it was a turning point in my life. I became so intrigued with theater that I changed my major from premed to drama. Eventually, I earned a B.A. in drama from Duke and an M.F.A. from FSU/Asolo Conservatory for Actor Training in Sarasota, Florida. Then, I began doing theater in New York. I also performed in regional shows around the country.

In 1993, after working in theater for several years, I met

Matthew Black, Matti. He was a musician with one of the shows I was doing. He wasn't an actor or a singer but a flat picker who played a Martin guitar. He had a beautiful voice but wasn't as comfortable singing as he was sitting on a stool in his jeans and his boots picking the guitar. Matti had blond, curly hair and the warmest, bluest eyes that you ever saw, and he was intense—in a good way. He was fully present when you were with him, like you were the most important person on the planet. His eyes could pierce right through you. We had a spiritual connection between us and fell deeply in love. Matti asked me to marry him in the spring of 1995, and I said "yes." We planned to have a simple wedding the following fall, but tragically Matti died from a complication with his medications a few months before the wedding.

He had been diagnosed as bipolar. Matti was up front with me from the beginning. I knew the score and wanted to do the journey with him because he was an amazing person and I loved him. I loved him so, so deeply. It was a love like I had never experienced before, and being the problem solver that I am, I was sure we could beat it.

We were living in Washington Heights, New York, by the George Washington Bridge, and I was working that night. We had plans to meet at the swing set on Twenty-Third Street, between Broadway and Fifth. Instead, I got a message from him saying that he couldn't meet. There was no explanation. It was such a beautiful night and I had my Rollerblades, so I strapped them on and started rolling home, just taking my time. When I got home, Matthew wasn't there, which I thought was odd.

I didn't get mad. Thank God, I didn't get mad. It was more like, "This is weird. Where is he?" Then, someone started laying on the buzzer, and I thought, *Matthew, come on. What are you doing?* I went over to the speaker and a man said, "This is the police, ma'am, can we please come up?"

Had Matti done something wrong or gotten into trouble? My heart pounded as I opened the door and stared at the two officers. "Okay, what'd he do?" I said, looking from one to the other.

"Who, ma'am?" one of them said.

"Matthew."

"Ma'am, do you know Matthew Black?"

"Yes," I said, "he's my fiancé."

"Ma'am, you need to come with us."

But why?

"There's not a lot we can tell you right now, but we found him on the side of the road, and we need you to come with us."

"Where are we going?"

"The hospital."

I wasn't panicked yet. But when they started running every traffic light, flying through, I started feeling really uneasy. They dropped me off at the emergency room, and I was told to sit in the waiting room. Later, I was brought to a little room about the size of a powder room and they started grilling me. "How do you know Matthew Black?"

"I'm his fiancée," I said.

"Does he have any kind of medical history?"

"Well," I said, "He's bipolar, so, yes, he's pretty sick. Can you please let me see him now?"

"Oh no, you don't understand; he's dead."

That was it. That's how they told me. I passed out right there on the floor of that hot, little room. For the next several days I was just numb, going through the motions of life. I was supposed to be going up to the Catskills to do a show, and the director called and asked me if I could still do it. As devastated as I was about Matti's death, I was afraid if I had too much time on my hands I would fall apart. I agreed to do the show because I had to have something to keep me occupied. We had a memorial service for Matti and spread his ashes.

It had started raining the day Matti died and hadn't let up. When I arrived at the actor housing in the Catskills it was still raining. All the actors were in rehearsal so I was alone. The place was beyond dreary. It was old and run-down, gray, and ugly. The linoleum on the floor was peeling. It was just the most depressing place. I had brought Matthew's Martin guitar and a few of his T-shirts and things, because I needed to have something of his near me. The guitar, of course, was his most prized possession.

The next day I went to rehearsal. When doing a show, you have rehearsal, and when you're not rehearsing, you do your life stuff. Well, I didn't have a life. I didn't have any life stuff to do. I had rehearsal, but then when rehearsal ended, I didn't have anything to attend to. With my emotions on a roller coaster, I picked up Matti's guitar just to feel it. I wanted so badly to be able to play because that was what we did together, we made music, and he was music and he had started me toward this dream of playing music and singing. He kind of brought the music alive in me when he was around, but without him I only knew how to play a few chords—G, D and A, or G, D and C. I could basically strum those chords, but it was very rough.

Even so, I began to write, strum, and sing what was going on inside of me. The first song I wrote was about the rain. I didn't intend to write songs; I just needed something to sing and those were the words that came out of me. The first words were, "And the rain keeps falling down / I don't know where I am going in this downpour." The rest of the song just poured out. Later, I called my friend and told her about the song, how it felt like part of my healing process, and she said, "Well, write another one." So I did.

As I got to know the cast and they learned what I was going through, they gave me space and were so kind. One night, they were all getting together and having drinks and invited me to join them. While we were on the porch, someone asked how I was doing and if they could help. I told them I was hanging in there.

They said, "We keep hearing the guitar. Do you play?"

"No. Not really. I mean, I fool with it," I said. "I don't know any songs. Just some that I've been writing."

Someone asked me to play, and I started singing the songs I'd written about Matti.

Once I began, it was like a dam opened up inside me. I realized that's what had been missing in my life—the connection, *the where* to flow to. When music flows out, it can't just flow out to nowhere. It has to flow to something, and these people were so receptive. As the music flooded out of me, I wrote several new songs. One was about jumping on a train, which is what Matti and I tried to do once. Another was called "New Shoes" and was about going home and finding all of Matti's things right where they belonged, including his pair of new shoes, but he wasn't there. The lyrics go like this:

Your new shoes are still sitting
In the middle of our bedroom floor
Your robe still hangs upon a hook
On the back of our bathroom door
And I know there'll come a day
When I put them all away
But for now, I need them there somehow

I'm at peace with the idea that it was your time to go
But was it my time to lose you is what I need to know
My friends all say you're with me forever now
Their words keep ringing in my ears: in spirit anyhow

I still sleep on the left side
Of our big old double bed
I whisper "Bear, I love you"
When all my prayers are said
I know there'll come a time

When I leave that all behind
But for now, I need it all somehow

I'm at peace with the idea that it was your time to go
But was it my time to lose you is what I need to know
My friends all say you're with me forever now
Their words keep ringing in my ears: in spirit anyhow

Your guitar is still perched upon its stand
And I haven't yet decided what to do with our wedding bands
But for now, I need them all somehow

And I'm at peace with the idea that it was your time to go
But was it my time to lose you is what I need to know
My friends all say you're with me forever now
Their words keep ringing in my ears: in spirit anyhow
My friends all say you're with me forever now
I believe them.
In spirit anyhow.

When I was back in New York, I went to a bar on Forty-Sixth Street on restaurant row where Matti and I had performed together. He had played the guitar and I sang backup for him. He was lined up to do another gig there. I had to tell the owner that Matti had died and couldn't do the show. His reaction was "Can you do it?" I was like, "No, I mean yes; of course I can do it." So I did. I had the three songs that I'd written about Matti, and I knew how to play "Me and Bobby McGee" and "Angel from Montgomery" (Matti's favorite song). I don't think I played either of them right, but they're only three chords, so it was hard to mess up. Between the songs, I filled it in with stories, trying to engage people.

When I finished, the people were clearly moved, even though most of them were there to drink beer and shoot pool. We all became this unit that night. My music really connected with them. I was moved. They were moved. It was like, "Wow, this is what I am meant to do."

You can have moments like that, and then it can go away and you forget. But I had these songs and I wanted to make a little tape to give to Matthew's family. I didn't even know how to record them. A friend of mine knew a musician who could help me. All of a sudden I had a record producer and an engineer who offered to record my songs on a CD with studio musicians for very little money. Of course, we went way past the hours we were allotted at the recording studio, but the guys were like, "We don't care. We're going to do this. This is cool." They were great. As fate would have it, some of the guys who heard me play had a connection with someone at *Billboard Magazine* and got my CD titled *New Shoes* to that person. *Billboard Magazine* reviewed it, loved it, and gave it the Critics' Choice for Best Newcomer. I've been making albums and touring the country ever since. That was more than a decade ago, and I'm still going strong.

On my new journey I met a guy named Peter Farrell. We connected too and make music together, just the two of us, me on the guitar and him on the piano or keyboard. And, oh, by the way, I married him. I guess if you're really lucky, real love does come around again. We have two children. Quinn, our youngest, is twenty-two months; and Clara, our daughter, is four and a half. So we're married and have children, and we're making the music of life together.

Meghan Cary's music has drawn comparisons to Shawn Colvin, Stevie Nicks, Blind Faith, and even Bruce Springsteen. An award-winning songwriter and a natural onstage, Cary was named *Billboard Magazine*'s Critics' Choice for Best Newcomer when she hit the music scene. As one critic exclaimed: "Cary is a star waiting to happen!" *(Barry Fox, Patriot-News)*. Check her out at www.MeghanCary.com.

100 Sounds to See

◆

Marsha Engle—Author, Wife, Mother, and Overcomer

"When circumstances are at their worst,
we can find our best."

—Elisabeth Kübler-Ross

How many people do you know who love their work? I did basically the same thing for twenty years and loved every minute of it. My job was primarily new product development in the health and beauty category. That's a fancy title for being an idea machine for shampoos, conditioners, skin care, and professional salon products.

Yes, that is what I did, day in and day out, for two decades. I snuck into the industry through the back door. Most people who have this job have an M.B.A. from a premier school. I had a nice undergraduate degree, but no traditional marketing training. What I did have was a track record of results. It was a career path with a few breaks and many years of hard work.

From the time I was a small child, I had a sensory neural hearing loss. For the most part, my life was relatively normal. Hearing aids and lip reading were the tools that allowed me to be a part of a fast-paced corporate environment. I could participate in meetings, and talking on the phone wasn't a problem. Other than a few "pardon me?" questions a day, my work was unaffected. Conversation was something I valued. I had to carefully lip-read what was being said to me, and as a result, I paid close attention.

I was a sponge for information, which helped me to develop a strong intuitive sense of what people wanted. No idea was ever really mine. My ideas came from the consumers who shared with me their frustrations, their likes, and also their hopes. Even though I was hearing impaired, I was a great listener.

I would stop people in stores and ask them about their purchases. Why are you buying that brand? What are your challenges with your hair? I thought nothing of interrogating a shop clerk in a Walgreens about what was selling. It wasn't unusual for conversations at the Thanksgiving dinner table to turn into a mini focus group on the hair-care needs of my friends and family.

I would hold little informal new product sessions with Girl Scouts, teaching them how to write a concept. I was impressed by the ideas that the kids would generate, their brilliance at creating something new and fresh. Their product suggestions were uninhibited since they weren't bridled by office politics or the fear of looking crazy.

In my offices at Clairol, Unilever, Alberto Culver (I worked for the best), I would grind out concepts that frequently turned into products. I was often seen cruising up and down the hall, asking my colleagues for feedback on an idea. Sometimes I drove my management a bit nuts. "How do you know that women need that product? You don't have research, data, to back up your thinking." Often, they would allow me to test my concept and many times they would score. *What a rush.* And then this idea might become a product in development. *What a thrill.* And sometimes the product would go on to be successful, taking share away from competitors. What a great way to make a living. Like I said earlier, I *loved* my job. So many great ideas, waiting to be discovered . . . all I had to do was listen. In my own small way, I was making the world a better place by giving people a better hair day.

When I decided to stay home with my little girl, my corporate job turned into a lucrative consulting business. Sometimes I would hit the computer during predawn hours, writing concepts and marketing plans for my clients, from a basement office. During the day, I had an amazing group of consumers to learn from—the moms at the playground. More time in the real world only made me better at what I was doing. The money was fantastic and the flexibility was great. Yes, I had it all. I was at home with my child, but I was still doing the job I loved. Also, there was an added bonus: I could sit in my bathrobe and eat Jelly Bellies while I worked.

Life was good. I had a loving husband, a darling little daughter, and a career on track. But in the back of my mind, I knew that a change would come. A change that I had no control over and the thought of it was so frightening, I pushed it away. I knew that my world would grow quiet, that someday I would be deaf.

In my late twenties, I was diagnosed with cochlear otosclerosis. This disease causes an overgrowth of cochlear bones, which leads to gradual nerve deafness. I was told that I would most likely be legally deaf by the age of forty. At the time of my diagnosis, I had just been offered a job in New York. It was a dream job, great money, a nice apartment, office on Park Avenue. Nobody was going to tell me that my life would have limitations. Skip that. I was twenty-seven years old, busy living, growing. It just wasn't going to be in my consideration set of trouble. Quite simply, I ignored it. Who wants to think about something as depressing as being deaf? Me? No, that wasn't going to happen. I was going to just stay hearing impaired. The doctors had to be wrong. I was a modern-day Scarlett O'Hara, "I'll think about that tomorrow." It wasn't a bad way to deal with it, because there was no cure. I just locked up this creepy idea of being deaf into a little box and pushed it to the very back of the shelf. But the box . . . it was there.

When the change began to happen, I was in my midforties. It wasn't too noticeable at first. I had trouble understanding the children who would come to play with my daughter. Their little voices were so soft, asking me for a snack or a toy. I was struggling a bit. Then talking on the phone became harder. Operators would get impatient with me as I strained to understand what was being said to me. So, I got a new hearing aid. Surely that was the problem.

Only the new hearing aid didn't help. It wasn't getting better. Conference calls with clients were disastrous. I simply couldn't understand what was being said to me. It sounded like everyone was talking inside a metal garbage can. The words were garbled and made no sense. Not understanding the content of the conversations was going to leave me in the dark. This was reflected in the quality of my work. I wasn't at the top of my game and I knew it.

My steady stream of work slowed to virtually nothing. I was fortunate that my husband's salary was enough for us to live on. But for me, it was never about the money. The money was nice, but what I loved was my work. I needed something to replace this career that I loved. I had all this creative energy and I wanted to be in touch with the outside world. I needed to reinvent my work.

I tried a little gig on eBay, thinking that I could create a business of recycled lighting and sell it to stores. Perfect! I didn't have to hear anyone, it was all online. Then all the eBay purchases started to roll in. The post office guy must have thought I was a bona fide nutcase. Let's put it this way, if there was a broken light available, it most likely ended up in my basement. Needless to say, it was a disaster. I ended up with a ton of busted lights and a nice balance on my credit card.

I had always been relatively successful. Failure was not something I had much experience with in my life. Failure sucks—especially when you are trying so hard to overcome something you have no control over. So, for the first time in my life, I felt sorry for myself. No one really knew. After I helped get everybody off and out of the house for the day, I would crawl under a big comforter on the couch. My dog would curl up at my feet. We would pass the day watching the captions of morning and afternoon TV. During those months, I saw many, many reruns of *Law and Order*. Because of the lack of activity, I gained weight. I had become numb, and numb was what I needed. If I couldn't do my work anymore, I would just hunker down under my comforter cocoon and insulate myself from what hurt.

During those dark days, the TV became my friend. The closed captions gave me a form of communication and I looked forward to my favorite shows. I would sit around all day watching TV, then right before my family came home I'd scramble to put the house in order and get dinner ready. It was not a good way to live and the depression wore on me. I had so many blessings in my life. I had a loving husband, a wonderful daughter, and together we lived in a comfortable home. "Surely this should be enough?" I asked myself. But my sadness and depression only grew into a full-blown grieving process.

Then one day, Oprah had a segment about a professor, Randy Pausch, who was delivering his "Last Lecture." I know that he inspired millions with his message. For me, it was far more than an inspiration; it was a wake-up call. It was time for me to get off the couch and begin living my life again. *What can I learn through this process of going deaf that will make me stronger? There has to be something for me to do with my days other than reclining on the couch.* Life is precious and I was wasting it. Professor Pausch's message of living like you mean it drilled through my numbness.

So I turned off the TV that day and decided that I would find my lesson in all of this. I would find something good, something worthwhile, something meaningful. Life as I knew it was not going to be the same. I had to reinvent myself. I wanted to work. I needed to find a way to use all this creative energy to make something. I wasn't going to get my answers by retreating. Randy Pausch said, "If you lead your life the right way, the karma will take care of itself. The dreams will come to you."

That is when I started praying. I have a beautiful back porch, surrounded by trees, that became my own private sanctuary. It was spring, and although I couldn't hear the sounds of this place, I could rest my eyes on the sights of trees blossoming . . . it was a place to heal. My prayer was a list of questions:

Dear God,
What am I supposed to learn from this?
What do you want me to do?
How can I stop feeling so sad?
What could I do that would give me the same rush, the
    same thrill that my work used to give me?

What would give me a sense of connection to the world
   and take away the isolation?
And finally, a few requests:
Help me not to be afraid.
Help me to accept the changes.
Help me to remember the sounds I could no longer hear.

Nothing happened right away. Until one day, I looked up in the trees and I could hear the birds—not with my ears, but with my eyes. By seeing those birds, I could remember the sound. I looked down at my dog panting at my feet and when I watched him, I could remember what a panting dog sounds like. I found this comforting. I have a good friend who is a professional photographer. I asked Bill if he would photograph sounds that I wished I could hear. I had a list of my own personal favorites. I missed the sound of rain on the roof, the wind in the trees, and the crunch of snow. But I also missed ordinary, uninteresting, everyday sounds like the snap of a green bean, the whistle of a teakettle, and the turn of a page.

The pictures started to come together and something else began to happen, too. I was creating something that gave me the same rush, the same thrill that my work once held. I realized that this little collection of pictures was something for the hearing world. It wasn't just about me anymore. Perhaps this book would serve as a reminder to the hearing world to listen to the sounds of a normal day.

I wrote a proposal for a book. Me? An author? Now, that is

something I would love to be. Yes, that filled many of my needs. It's kind of like developing new products—lots of writing and thinking. I'm creating something from nothing and really like that. Writing gives me a sense of collaboration and cuts off the isolation. Finally, it gave me a new career. I'm a writer.

Remember those prayers? Well, if you know anything about the publishing world these days, getting published is no easy feat. Also, remember, I was unknown and had never published anything except the copy on the back of the shampoo bottle in your shower. It was going to take God answering a prayer to make this happen. I have written countless marketing plans over the years. Book proposals are very similar, so this came pretty easily to me. I sent the proposal to only one agent, Kristina, who had come highly recommended to me. Then I waited for several weeks.

When Kristina accepted me as a client, I was overjoyed. There I was, virtually unknown, and I had landed this wonderful agent. We made a fantastic team. Her guidance and expertise helped me to fine-tune my proposal. Once we were both happy with the product, she sent it off to several strong publishers. And, once again, I waited.

It wasn't very long before Carol, an editor at HCI Books, lovingly adopted the project. She was another wonderful person who would help make my idea a reality. Suddenly, it felt just like it used to when I was in my former career, working with a team of people to create something new. Only this time, it held a far greater importance than a revolutionary conditioner. It was my story and also my lesson.

As I write this essay, lying on my desk in front of me is *100 Sounds to See,* a beautiful little purple book containing 100 stunning photographs taken by my friend Bill Huber with suggestive captions that elicit the memory of a sound. HCI invited me to the printing plant a few weeks ago to see *100 Sounds to See* come off the press. It was so much like those days before, when I would watch a hair-care product roll off the high-speed line on the factory floor. A product that I had nurtured from a concept on paper to a formula in a bottle, this little book gave me the same thrill, the same rush.

I held the book in my hands and looked at the faces of the people at HCI who were making it happen. If they only knew how slippery the slope was back in those days when I had to wait for those prayers to be answered.

So, here I am with work I love, all new and yet somewhat the same. When someone asks me, "What do you do?" I tell them, "I am a writer." I am an author . . . and I like the sound of that.

Marsha Engle is the author of *100 Sounds to See.* She is busily working on her next writing project. She lives with her husband, Mark Reinecke, a professor at Northwestern University Medical School, and their daughter, Gracie, in Geneva, Illinois.

If She Can Succeed . . .

◆

Madam C. J. Walker—Child of Freed Slaves and First Woman Self-Made Millionaire

"If you keep doing what you've always done, you'll always get what you've always gotten."

—John C. Maxwell

Life in rural Louisiana in 1867 was not easy, especially for Sarah Breedlove. Her parents had been slaves, but were freed only to become sharecroppers, which created its own form of slavery and poverty. By the age of seven both of Sarah's parents had died in a sweeping epidemic of yellow fever, leaving her orphaned and illiterate. Sarah and her sister were forced to work six days a week, from daylight to dark, picking cotton. At age ten, because of a failing crop along the Mississippi River Delta, Sarah and her sister moved up the river to Vicksburg and took jobs as maids in white households. She married at age fourteen to escape an abusive situation but was widowed by twenty. Again she moved, this time to St. Louis with her two-year-old daughter to be closer to family. There, she worked as a washerwoman for a little more than a dollar per day. "I was at my tubs one morning with a heavy wash before me. As I bent over the washboard and looked at my arms buried in soapsuds, I said to myself, 'What are you going to do when you grow old and your back gets stiff? Who is going to take care of your little girl?' This set me to thinking, but with all my thinking I couldn't see how I, a poor washerwoman, was going to better my condition."[1]

Life had not been good to Sarah. Yet, despite adversity that most of us will fortunately never know, she refused to give in to the victim mentality. With unswerving courage and resolve, she tapped into the same energy source that resides in all of us and gave herself a do over. Transcending her past, she educated herself and her daughter and became known as Madam C. J. Walker, who, according to Guinness World Records was the first self-made female millionaire—white or black—in the United States.

How could someone in her situation pull off such a feat? To start with, Sarah Breedlove was a person of action. She was well acquainted with the principle that nothing happens until something moves. One day at age thirty-five she had a moment of self-revelation and took action on that revelation. At that time, the home Sarah lived in had no indoor plumbing or electricity. Because of poor facilities, like many women of that era, she only washed her hair occasionally—usually, about once a month. This

---

[1] Brian Souza, *Become Who You Were Born to Be* (New York: Harmony Books, 2005), 47.

brought about severe dandruff and scalp disease that caused Sarah's hair to begin falling out, resulting in near baldness. It was then that she had a flash of inspiration for a line of hair-care products. She later told reporters that the idea for her Wonderful Hair Grower product had come to her in a dream. She dreamed of a man who came and told her the ingredients needed for the mixture to grow back her hair. After the dream, Sarah mixed the ingredients up in her bathtub, tried it out on herself, and discovered it worked.

But ideas mean nothing without action. Like all successful do overs, Sarah knew she needed to step out of her comfort zone and take a chance on herself. In 1905, she did just that. With only $1.50 in her pocket, she moved to Denver, Colorado, where she took a job working for another black woman who manufactured hair-care products. It was there that she began to further develop her own products and sell them. These products grew out hair that had been lost and helped soften and straighten the hair of African American women. During this time she remarried and changed her name to Madam C. J. Walker. Walker was her husband's name, but she gave herself the name Madam to add a touch of class to her products, which she called Madam C. J. Walker's Wonderful Hair Grower, Madam C. J. Walker's Glossine, and Madam C. J. Walker's Vegetable Shampoo.

In the early 1900s, few women, let alone African American women, traveled solo. Undaunted, Madam C. J. roamed the highways and byways across the country spreading the word about her products. In the beginning, she sold them door-to-door, then through the mail, and ultimately in pharmacies. But she always held faithfully to her vision, increasingly sought ways to better herself and her business, and was unyielding in her marketing efforts.

In addition to developing her unique gifts and business, Madam C. J. poured herself into the development of other black women worldwide, creating well-paying jobs for them, helping them gain confidence, self-respect, and business savvy.

It's hard to comprehend that Madam C. J. Walker had once been an impoverished, illiterate, orphan, picking cotton in Louisiana with the bleakest of futures. Yet, she never gave in to self-despair or self-pity. Instead, she stayed humble and focused, willing to do whatever it took, including taking the most menial of jobs if necessary. Her do-over journey from the sharecropping fields of Louisiana to being a leader for empowering women and economic freedom is not only amazing, but it's significant for us and our lives as well. "Perseverance is my motto," she once said. "It laid the Atlantic cable; it gave us the telegraph, telephone, and wireless. It gave to the world Abraham Lincoln and to the race, freedom."[2] At the National Negro Business League Convention in 1912, she said, "I am a woman who came from the cotton fields of the South. From there I was promoted to the washtub. From there I was promoted to the cook-kitchen. And from there I promoted myself into the business of

---

[2] Ibid., 48.

manufacturing hair goods and preparations . . . I have built my own factory on my own ground."

In the words of her biographer Beverly Lowry, "Madam C. J. Walker was an icon, a legend, and an exemplar." We can learn much from her.

Sources

Lowry, Beverly. *Her Dream of Dreams: The Rise and Triumph of Madam C. J. Walker.* New York: Alfred A. Knopf, 2003.
Bundles, A'Lelia. *On Her Own Ground: The Life and Times of Madam C. J. Walker.* New York: Scribner, 2001.
Souza, Brian. *Become Who You Were Born to Be.* New York: Harmony Books, 2005.

From Disappointment to Reappointment

♦

Tessa Simmons—Teacher of Special Needs Children

"True success consists not in becoming
the person you dreamed of becoming when
you were young, but in becoming the
person you were meant to be . . ."

—Rabbi Harold S. Kushner

At age thirteen, my mother died, leaving in my life a void that made my teenage years hard. Fortunately, I had a special aunt who became a pillar in my life. I spent many days and nights visiting her home. I can remember my aunt's home as a place of love and warmth, filled with delightful aromas forever seeping out from the kitchen, infiltrating the entire house. She was a stay-at-home mom and a masterful homemaker. When visiting, I'd often gaze at her from a distance and dream of one day being a homemaker just like her, living in a warm and loving home just like hers. Growing up, this was my vision of how life was going to be for me—of how life "should" be. I was going to marry Prince Charming, have children, and build a wonderful family home.

That was my dream and I did indeed find my "Prince Charming." Just as I imagined, we got married and started building our dream home. All was seemingly well until he became addicted to alcohol and drugs and I found out he was being unfaithful to me. The news devastated me. Of course, after I confronted him, he promised to change, but his chemical abuse and unfaithfulness continued. Soon, I found myself on my own as a single mom with three children—my perfect little world shattered. To make matters worse, I had no career to fall back on because all my life I'd prepared to be a homemaker. The breakup of my marriage hit me hard, and I fought continual bouts of overwhelming depression and fear. As a result, I lost an unhealthy amount of weight. Life seemed dark and hopeless. During that time, I wrote a letter to myself that expressed my feelings. I'd like to share it with you.

Tonight, the girls and I decorated the Christmas tree. We spent the evening frolicking around the tree farm in search of that perfect tree with the most fluff. I sampled every one of them and was sure that we had picked the one that smelled the most like Christmas.

Driving home was fun; the girls giggled as we passed cars on the street with our tree sticking two feet out of the trunk of the car. Now, after angel kisses and reprimands for feeding cheddar crackers to Gabby, the dog, they sleep peacefully. I sneaked upstairs to release the tears that I've held back all evening.

This is the second Christmas that the kids and I have spent alone without their daddy. This is the time of year for families, and my heart longs for us to be together. Although that longing is inside of me, I know that my health and my children's future depend upon my being strong. It's a tough fight, but giving in to that longing would just bring more unbearable pain and ultimate destruction. I've learned that doing what's right sometimes means standing alone, and I've found that being alone isn't nearly as painful as being lonely. . . . Sometimes the anger and hurt overwhelm me.

Because of my children and eventually for me, I knew I had to do something. I just couldn't continue to live in a pit of despair and poverty. Frantically, I cried out to God for direction. I had to provide for my children and find a new purpose for my life. I had to reinvent myself. I needed a do over in the most critical sense.

In the past, I had entertained the idea of teaching school on the elementary level, but the opportunity never arose. After my divorce, however, I was free to pursue teaching. The only catch was I'd have to go to college and I was in my midthirties, raising three kids, with no money! The impossibility of my situation loomed over me like a big, dark cloud. It took humbling myself to accept my father's offer for my children and me to move in with him. After the move, I enrolled in college with great determination. Having a loving and supportive family who helped with the kids and allowed us to stay in their home was a major factor in my recovery process. Going back to school built up my self-confidence. My old dream of being the perfect wife, mother, and homemaker died. It was actually dead long before I was able to let it go. To move forward in a healthy way, I had to develop a new dream.

I knew that I had certainly made mistakes in my past. Now I wanted to do more than just not make the same mistakes again. I resolved to myself, *I'm going to find out how to do things "right" this time.* Thus began my journey to find out how to have a successful, "normal" life, if I could just find out what normal was.

At this point, I'd given up the pursuit of having a healthy romantic relationship. I had been betrayed once and that was enough. I never wanted to feel that kind of pain again. I wanted to be my own woman now and determine my own path. My resolve to be a loving mother never changed, but my dream had switched from being a quaint homemaker to being a successful teacher. My grades were high, and I worked diligently and passionately. My confidence soared. I just knew I was going to be a wonderful teacher. After all, I was attending one of the best elementary-education schools in the state, and I had a deep love for children. Who wouldn't want to hire me?

Envisioning my future as a teacher, in my mind, I pictured a traditional classroom, just like in the movies—decorated in bright primary colors, with neat children who said, "Gooood moooornnnning, Ms. Tessa!" All smart kids, with caring and involved parents, eager and willing to learn, like little sponges soaking up all the knowledge I would give them.

After graduation, though, I couldn't find a job. I searched and scoured, but nothing opened up. Finally, out of desperation, I interviewed at an inner-city school located in a crime-ridden, drug-infested part of town and was hired to teach the first grade. It was the only job offered to me, so I had to take it.

When I began teaching, once again my vision of what life "should be" was shattered. Most of these kids come to school with no supplies. Their parents were in dire poverty. At first, they didn't want to learn. I had to spend hours teaching them how to behave, before I could teach them anything else. Many of my students' parents were in jail. A significant percent were crack babies, which causes super-hyperactivity. One of them brought a gun to school—in the first grade! Another one had ringworms and had patches the size of cup lids all over his body.

Each day after work I cried. I bought newspapers and continued diligently to look for a new job. But it was as though a steel door had been slammed shut. There were just no jobs to be had. Again, in desperation, I prayed, "God, I can't do this! I went to college for nothing. If I can't do this, then I can't do anything!"

I felt like a total failure. My marriage had failed and now I failed as a teacher, and I didn't want to step foot back into the classroom. I was so miserable and I was driving those around me crazy. Facing each new day became harder and harder until one day I came to the end of my rope, again.

Then, almost miraculously, a light switched on in my head. It occurred to me that I was trying to fit my students into my expectation of what "normal" was supposed to be. With new resolve, I determined not to give up on my job just yet, or on my students, but to press on. After a while, I was the one who began to change. It wasn't the children who needed to grow; it was me. I started seeing my students as individuals, with unique problems. I was the only person some of these kids had who offered them any positive emotional support.

I implemented a system in which at the beginning of each day every student had to greet me by shaking my hand, slapping a high five, or giving me a hug. In the beginning, most of the kids were emotionally guarded because too many people in their lives had let them down, and most didn't want anything to do with touching me. However, through continual praise and offering unconditional acceptance, they slowly began to open up. Now, almost every one of them gives me, not high fives, but hugs. Some don't want to let me go. It may be the only hug they get all day. But they had to learn to trust me.

I saw such a change in my students and myself that I now know beyond a shadow of a doubt that God took my idealistic dream of teaching and turned it into a very realistic *mission* to love these children in need. The principal of the school told me one day that God had sent me to the school. It's true. Yes, God put me in that school, but it was as much for me as it was for them. I gained so much wisdom during my time there. And little did I know it was preparation for what I am doing today, helping children with learning disabilities.

Oh, I still had my bad days. But at the end of each day I started having the peace that comes with knowing that I was exactly where I was supposed to be. Instead of crying like I used to, I laughed a lot. What I've learned, and what I'm filtering down to my students, is that life is about risks. We don't always know the outcome, but regardless of our past or present situations, we must have the self-confidence to step out.

My classroom was and is not what I envisioned in college and there's always a shortage of funding, but my life is more rewarding than it has ever been. In my classroom, as in my personal life, I realized I have to take leaps of faith, which means trusting people and God again.

I know there are no guarantees, but I also know if I am a whole person, secure in myself, then I will always make it. That gives me great hope for the future—a realistic hope. I know from experience that God can take our broken dreams and unfulfilled expectations and use them. Then our lives will be complete. I still have disappointments and pain, but instead of giving up, I'm learning to dream new dreams and let the old ones fade into memory.

After spending several years working with inner-city children and letting them and the experience grow her, Tessa has developed the teaching skills that enable her to further specialize in children with learning disabilities. Though it's often difficult and her past frequently comes back to haunt her, with the help of God and the support of her family, she's overcoming.

Shoulder to Shoulder with Success

◆

Kathleen Kirkwood—Former Model, Designer, and Entrepreneur

"We have more possibilities available in
each moment than we realize."

—Thich Nhat Hanh

At the age of nineteen, after twelve years of attending Catholic
school in Valley Stream, New York, and a short stint at Albany
College, I decided to venture into New York City and give modeling a shot. Fortunately, one thing led to another, and within a
year, I had landed a $60,000 minimum yearly contract with the
Ford Modeling Agency, the largest modeling agency in the
world. It was the late 1970s and sixty grand was a lot of money!

Ford planned to send me to Paris, and an American in Paris
was a better "sell" than staying here and competing locally. In
America they want the European look, and in Europe, they want
the American look. Whatever you're not, that's what they want.
I had been to Paris several times, so could not wait to land, get

situated in the company apartment, and begin my journey to stardom. I had the airline tickets and was ready to go.

My dream was becoming a reality. What could go wrong, right? Well, the day before I was supposed to fly to Paris I was crossing the street at the corner of 53rd and 2nd Avenue and the car making a right turn stopped for the "pedestrians' right of way." Evidently, the car behind him was impatient and zipped around trying to pass, and in the process, hit me while I was still crossing. The impact sent me flying over the hood of the car like a stunt woman and slammed me down on the unforgiving asphalt; I actually remember visualizing Burt Reynolds' car stunts, to roll up the hood and roll back to the ground. If I ever get to meet him one day, I will have to thank him personally for all his movie stunts, which could have saved my life.

Amazingly, I didn't break any bones, but the car struck my leg, causing a deep hematoma (a permanent lump). Needless to say, on that day, I missed my flight to Paris. I missed everything. The agency basically said, "Because you have a permanent bump on your leg we can't support the contract (in other words, 'You're done')." It was irreparable damage, so the contract was breached. There wasn't a lot of back-and-forth. That's how the business works.

Even though it seemed like my whole world had come to an end, I wasn't going to give up on my dream just yet. But in order to continue pursuing modeling I would have to take a step down and try for smaller jobs. At that time, my claim to fame was disco roller skating. I was good, and department stores like Macy's and

Bloomingdale's would hire me to do roller-skating expos for their fashion products. Another job was working for Richard Donner, the director and producer of the *Superman* and *Lethal Weapon* movies. His team wanted the Superman jackets showcased at retailers and they hired me to roller skate in a Supergirl jacket at his events, promoting the movie. *Superman* was heavily advertised and I had become the "iconic" Superman roller-mascot. . . . I was so well known for skating at the time that the pop band Hall & Oates hired me for their video "Portable Radio," which someone downloaded recently on YouTube. What a shock to see yourself thirty years later on YouTube . . . but there I was, skating in Central Park in the video.

Fast forward: It was the early 1980s and shoulder pads were a huge part of women's fashion. *However, you couldn't just buy the shoulder pads.* You had to buy the whole outfit. It was the same regardless of the designer—Thierry Mugler, Claude Montana, Norma Kamali, or whoever—they were not offered separately. Because of the scenario that I just described, I didn't have much cash to be a fashion plate. Yet I did have an eye for fashion and determined, after pining over a $1,000 jacket . . . *What I'm really liking about that jacket are the shoulder pads.*

So I detached the pads from one of my outfits and created a little Velcro strip that I used to attach to my bra. I could then use the pads for all my outfits, even my roller-skating outfits. When I'd go to the gym, or the changing room, or anyplace, women would see what I had done and jealously exclaim, "That's fabulous. Where can we get those?"

When I'd say, "Oh, I just sewed them together," women would offer to buy them from me, right off my shoulders!

Because so many women were asking me to part with my pads, I came up with a packaging idea—why not an ice cream pint? Shoulder pads made a woman look "thinner" so the "Pint" would be sweet revenge for the fattening contents it usually contained . . . I trademarked Pints-of-Pads and decided to start my own business. In the beginning I went searching for a factory and nobody wanted to give me the time of day, much less give someone so young any financing or credit. Every factory told me that it was just a ridiculous concept. Get this picture: I'm twenty-one years old, and I'm walking into these huge factories saying, "Hello, I'd like you to manufacture my designer, attachable shoulder pads and put them in a pint of ice cream package." Most of my friends and family were convinced my gray matter had melted (except my dad, who thought it was genius; Mom thought it was cool, too). Finally, after much persistence, I found a factory in New York that agreed to make my first "batch" if I prepaid for everything. It just so happened that I'd received a $20,000 settlement from the car accident, and after living off most of that, I took the remaining $5,000 to buy my first shipment of shoulder pads and pint containers.

I told Richard Donner, the Hollywood producer, about my business, just to see if he got a laugh about what his Superman roller skater was up to. After I told him my story, he said, "You're about the gutsiest twenty-one-year-old I've ever met. Most women I meet your age want a part in a movie, but you want to share a business plan!" He had his "set director" place one of my pints in the *Lethal Weapon 2* bathroom scene (think Danny Glover about to explode off the bog), and invited me to all the *Lethal Weapon* opening events where I would give out my Pints-of-Pads. That's how I met the original crew of *Saturday Night Live* and Gilda Radner. They all went crazy for them.

From there, I called Bloomingdale's and said, "Hi, I invented the first clip-on shoulder pad, and they've appeared in *Lethal Weapon*. . . ." They gave me an appointment and bought sixty pieces. In those days, the shipping was different than it is today. The order was written by hand on a piece of paper. There were no computers, no e-mail or electronic anything. I lived ten blocks away and delivered the order to Bloomingdale's in person (yes, the 60th Street loading dock). They sold out in one weekend! It was crazy because prior to that, shoulder pads were a sewing notions product. It was an extra little item that cost about sixty cents. The thought of someone paying ten dollars for a pair in a Pint was outrageous, but the look, for fashionistas at the time, was close to an addiction. Which is funny because my tagline and first MTV commercial was "Get hooked." My hook was the Velcro attachment.

Once I sold Bloomingdale's, I was swamped with overnight orders from places like Nieman Marcus, Saks Fifth Avenue, and Macy's. I was the only one with a shoulder pad concept, and retailers would track me down and fax me incredible orders. Within a two-year period I was shipping about $2.5 million while still living in my walk-up tenement apartment on 64th Street!

The growth continued, and over the next two decades millions of Pints-of-Pads were sold. Eventually I had to expand my manufacturing by adding factories to keep up with the demand. I printed them in three languages, French, Spanish, and Japanese. My business was featured in the *Wall Street Journal* and *Fortune* magazine. I was on *Oprah, Regis Philbin,* and even Joan Rivers's *Can We Shop?* show. Then, around 1991, the eighties fashion thing was wearing down and shoulder pads really took a dive. However, I had a huge following and was making a great living. The whirlwind of the eighties was over, but what remained was still steady.

One day I was reading a copy of the *Women's Wear Daily* newspaper and there was an ad in the back that said, "Television show looking for product." Being curious and always looking to promote my products, I called. It turned out to be a new little cable company called QVC, offering TV shopping products. I really didn't even know what it was, but I went on the show with ninety of my Pints and sold out in just a short period. Kathy Levine was my first show host, and I've been on QVC ever since, almost twenty years later. CNBC recently filmed a reality segment of my process on QVC; they came to my house with the camera crew and followed me to QVC and recorded a "behind-the-scenes" on-air appearance, which was an absolute ball for me.

Since that time, my shoulder pad factory in Asia, a great innovator, developed a very technical one-piece bra that became the largest selling bra of all time for companies such as Victoria's Secret and Wacoal. I've been able to partner with this Asian innovator and tap into his groundbreaking techniques, adding our laser-cut Ultrasonic Shapewear on the "Q," trademarked Sonic Slimmers. Now, for the first time, I'm able to experience new classes of exposure with items featured as a QVC Today's Special Value and full Kathleen Kirkwood Wardrobe Solution Shows, something I was not able to with the limitations of shoulder pads. Every day has been a new success at QVC—a company that truly understands how and when to support an entrepreneur like myself.

As I mentioned, my father was also a huge supporter. He once said to me, "Kathleen, you have an entrepreneurial spirit. You're constantly inventing things. You can't help it. It's who you are" *(That's true. If I go through a day without creating a new product in my mind, it would be a rare day).* I've been this way since I could speak. In the beginning, every time I'd come home and say, "Hey, here's my new business idea," my family would roll their eyes and say, "Here comes another crazy idea from Kathleen." At the end of the conversation, they would tell me, "Just get a nice job. Be a dental hygienist or something."

But the weekend I came home with my shoulder pad business plan and told my father, it stopped him in his tracks. He was a Wall Street guy, a clever man. He looked at me and said, "Kathleen, that's the best idea I've ever heard—you're either going to fail or you're going to make a trillion. The idea is so good that if you don't quit and start your Pints-of-Pads, I'm going to quit E. F. Hutton to do it myself because it's that good!" He had never reacted that way. He'd always advised me to "play it safe," "keep my job," and "do it after work, or on the weekend" and "first try and see." So when my father reacted so enthusiastically, it really gave me the extra little bit of confidence I needed to take the leap of faith. For you to reinvent your life and make your dream a reality requires taking some leaps of faith, often in the face of ridicule. There's really no other way.

If somebody is thinking about pursuing their entrepreneurial dream, I would say the hardest thing to do is to quit your job and start. In my opinion, when you make your dream full time, you leave no room for error. You are forced to make it. I've heard many people try to start their company on the side after their day job . . . I don't think you can really create a viable venture, effectively, from 5:00 PM to midnight after working all day. Stepping out on your own is the biggest risk you will ever take because the odds are you'll fail. For me, losing my modeling contract really became a blessing in disguise because it forced me to get creative. There came a point, though, in order to really make the business work, I had to let go of other things and focus my energy on it full time. I had no place to go, I guess sink or swim—luckily the pads were buoyant! I was pouring my heart and soul into it every day. Bottom line: if you feel the idea is worth taking the risks, then chances are you'll beat the odds.

To learn more about Kathleen Kirkwood and her company ForEverYoung, visit www.Kathleenkirkwood.com.

READER/CUSTOMER CARE SURVEY

HEFG

We care about your opinions! Please take a moment to fill out our online Reader Survey at **http://survey.hcibooks.com.**
As a **"THANK YOU"** you will receive a **VALUABLE INSTANT COUPON** towards future book purchases
as well as a **SPECIAL GIFT** available only online! Or, you may mail this card back to us.

First Name		MI.	Last Name	

Address			City	

State		Zip	Email	

1. Gender
❑ Female ❑ Male

2. Age
❑ 8 or younger
❑ 9-12 ❑ 13-16
❑ 17-20 ❑ 21-30
❑ 31+

3. Did you receive this book as a gift?
❑ Yes ❑ No

4. Annual Household Income
❑ under $25,000
❑ $25,000 - $34,999
❑ $35,000 - $49,999
❑ $50,000 - $74,999
❑ over $75,000

5. What are the ages of the children living in your house?
❑ 0 - 14 ❑ 15+

6. Marital Status
❑ Single
❑ Married
❑ Divorced
❑ Widowed

7. How did you find out about the book?
(please choose one)
❑ Recommendation
❑ Store Display
❑ Online
❑ Catalog/Mailing
❑ Interview/Review

8. Where do you usually buy books?
(please choose one)
❑ Bookstore
❑ Online
❑ Book Club/Mail Order
❑ Price Club (Sam's Club, Costco's, etc.)
❑ Retail Store (Target, Wal-Mart, etc.)

9. What subject do you enjoy reading about the most?
(please choose one)
❑ Parenting/Family
❑ Relationships
❑ Recovery/Addictions
❑ Health/Nutrition
❑ Christianity
❑ Spirituality/Inspiration
❑ Business Self-help
❑ Women's Issues
❑ Sports

10. What attracts you most to a book?
(please choose one)
❑ Title
❑ Cover Design
❑ Author
❑ Content

TAPE IN MIDDLE; DO NOT STAPLE ||||

BUSINESS REPLY MAIL

FIRST-CLASS MAIL PERMIT NO 45 DEERFIELD BEACH, FL

POSTAGE WILL BE PAID BY ADDRESSEE

Health Communications, Inc.
3201 SW 15th Street
Deerfield Beach FL 33442-9875

FOLD HERE

Comments

When Your Dream Becomes Your Call

♦

Max Davis—Author, Speaker, and Encourager

"The dark threads were as needful,
in the weaver's skillful hand, as the threads of gold
and silver, for the pattern which he planned."

—Anonymous

Eighteen years ago I was cruising through life. Upbeat and oozing with confidence, I was one of the most positive guys you'd ever meet. I had been successful at nearly everything I'd put my hands to—voted "Most Athletic" and "Friendliest" in high school, played football in college on a full scholarship, made the dean's list, and because I wanted to serve God all out, continued to seminary after undergraduate school to prepare for full-time service in the ministry. On the way, I got married and had two beautiful children—a precious girl, Kristen, and a curly-headed boy, James. Then, finally, after years of preparation and waiting, I was ordained a pastor of my own church that I felt certain God had called me to. Life was great. God was with me. What could go wrong? Right?

Because I was doing God's work, I threw myself passionately into the church doing counseling, hospital visitation, home visitation, preaching, cleaning, and even leading song service because I could play the guitar. I was blessed. The problem was, I felt I had to have my hand in everything so I could be in control. And I was serving everyone but my own family. As strange as it may seem, though I was a minister and said I was serving God, my life was about me. I was growing a great church. I was going to be a great preacher. I was going to be a good counselor. I, I, I—all in the name of God. There was no doubt that I loved God, but still, my life was about me. Plus, I had become pretty good at pushing things that I didn't want to deal with under the rug.

The church was growing by leaps and bounds. I had a beautiful home in a quaint college town. On the surface everything was smiles, but I could sense things around the house were not right. I couldn't put my finger on what was wrong. There was tension in the air. When I thought about it, I would quickly dismiss the thought and say things to myself like, "Everything's okay. It must be because you're doing God's work." But things were not okay. Storm clouds were gathering on the horizon, and I continued to ignore them. Then one day the kids and I came home to an empty house. My wife had left me. It felt like someone had kicked me in the stomach. A wave of nausea swept over me. I wanted to throw up. After regrouping emotionally, I figured, "Okay. I get the message. I'll do whatever it takes and fix this."

But, long story short, she didn't come back and the marriage wasn't healed.

We were living in Lawrence, Kansas, at the time and Kansas had a sixty-day no-fault divorce rule. Within sixty days, I found myself divorced, separated from my kids whom I dearly loved, out of the ministry that I had spent years preparing for, and completely ruined financially. I'd given my life to serve God and felt He'd stood idly by while my whole life came crashing down.

Even though many of the people in the church did not want me to step down, the denomination we were a part of figured it would be best if I did in order to focus on my healing. To their credit, I was an emotional basket case and in no shape to lead. The problem was, the church was my income and now that was gone too. They took up a small collection but it only helped for the short term—the very short term. My first priority was Kristen and James. I was not going to abandon them, so I stayed in the area even though the job market was incredibly difficult. Plus, have you ever tried to switch careers and your life path when you are emotionally devastated?

For more than a year I was so broke that I couldn't even afford an efficiency apartment and lived with several different sets of friends who knew my plight. At times, I was reduced to sleeping in my car—a twelve-year-old, burnt-orange, rusting Toyota. Once, a policeman woke me up by tapping on the car window with the butt of his flashlight and told me to get moving.

There were nights I would spend curled up on the floor in the fetal position, broken, humiliated, hurting, overwhelmed with shame, on the verge of a nervous breakdown, crying out to a God whom I was certain had no more use for me. For the longest time, I couldn't even set foot in a church because I felt angry and betrayed, but still, I continued to cry out to God. I didn't even know what to pray, so quite often my prayer was simply, "GOD!" Once, I was driving down the interstate at night and because of the overwhelming sense of anguish, I had to pull the car over, get out, and pace back and forth crying, "God!" until I found the strength to continue.

◆ ◆ ◆ ◆

One day I was walking down Massachusetts Street in Lawrence. It was cold and I was hungry and had no money. I mean *no* money. Sick of borrowing from friends and relatives, I'd gone through a series of jobs trying to sell vacuum cleaners and cars but couldn't give them away. I may have been the world's worst vacuum cleaner salesman. Looking back, I was so distraught emotionally it was affecting everything I did. I was like a walking zombie overwhelmed with failure, pain, and low self-esteem. I'm sure I was repelling people and potential buyers. That particular day I was walking down the street with tears streaming down my face and I began to pray. "Lord, I believe you are real. My whole life is based on that belief. I'm hungry, God. Please make a way and provide for me . . ." Just as I finished saying those words, I looked out of the corner of my eye, and I kid you not, there was a twenty-dollar bill stuck in the gutter. I reached down and picked it up, thanking God for His provision. The food never tasted better that day. But here's where the story gets really wild. The next day, I was broke again and prayed the same prayer while walking down the same street. This time when I finished my prayer I saw a ten-dollar bill! My office had been located on that street, and I had walked it dozens if not hundreds of times in the past and never found a single dime. Now, twice in two days while praying for daily food, I found money. Let me ask you, when was the last time you found a twenty-dollar bill on the sidewalk? Some people may chalk that up to mere coincidence, but I just couldn't. It was just too bizarre. God was getting my attention. He was sending me a message and the message was, though I didn't understand what was going on in my life or why, and I didn't know what my future held, God knew exactly where I was and He had not abandoned me.

That day was a turning point. From that moment on I began living my life one day at a time, simply putting one foot in front of the other, desperately depending on God to carry me through my circumstances. I stopped blaming others for my problems, stopped seeing myself as a victim, and began working on my own self-defeating behaviors. At times it was ugly and I saw a lot of stuff in myself that made me cringe, but after a while an amazing thing began to happen. Day by day, month by month, step by step, little by little, I began to grow and transform into a different person. Though my outward circumstances had not changed, freedom and joy were slowly replacing despair and self-loathing. Healing was taking place. My confidence was growing again, but this time it was a confidence based on total dependence on God instead of myself.

Both my ex-wife and I were from Louisiana, and when she eventually moved back I followed to be close to my two children. Humbled, broken, and poor, I moved back in with my parents. My parents! I had gone from "Most Athletic" to "Most Pathetic"! As my healing and confidence continued to grow, I began to rebuild and try to figure out what to do with the rest of my life. For years I had entertained the dream of being a writer. In fact, I had majored in journalism in college and received a master's degree because I believed that one day I would be a writer. Yet, I never had the guts or time to actually go for it all out and make that dream a reality.

After a while, as I got back on my feet, I ran into an old high school friend named Alanna whom I had dated and had been absolutely crazy about. To be perfectly honest, because I figured she was way out of my league back in high school, surely she would be out of my league now that I was broke and feeling lower than a snake's belly. I can't believe she turned out to be my soul mate, my best friend, and my partner in life. We've been happily married for seventeen years! We live in a peaceful little home in the country with a big off-the-ground front porch surrounded by oak trees, pine trees, and camellia plants. We even have peacocks walking around our yard! It's truly a writer's paradise. I can't imagine being any happier. How Alanna and I reconnected and wound up married is a whole different story that I could write a book about. Maybe I will one day.

When Alanna and I started seeing each other again, I shared with her my dream of writing, and in a sarcastic, yet genuinely honest spirit she told me, "You ought to just go for it because you can't get any lower than you are now. What do you have to lose?" She was right: when you've got nothing, you've got nothing to lose. And I had all the time in the world. So I took her advice!

Because I figured no one would publish my first book, I published it myself and it was most definitely an adventure. I literally loaded the books in the back of my car and sold them store-to-store, door-to-door, and by telemarketing. If you were breathing and you met me, you got pitched a book. This was something I would have never lowered myself to do before. But I was desperate, and desperation is some pretty good motivation. Failure was not an option. That attitude paid off. My little self-published book titled *Never Stick Your Tongue Out at Mama & Other Life-Transforming Revelations* sold around 10,000 copies in my area, which was almost unheard of for a self-published book.

Eventually, the book caught the eye of a top New York agent and then the largest New York publisher in the world! It got a half page in the *USA Today* newspaper, and I began doing book signings, television interviews, and speaking engagements all over. Thus, my career as a writer had begun, and here I am sixteen books later. A few of my other titles are *It's Only a Flat Tire in the Rain: Navigating Life's Bumpy Roads with Faith and Grace; Desperate Dependence: When You Reach the End, God's Best Begins;* and *Luke's Passage* (my first novel).

I want to be careful, however, not to mislead anyone. Though the road has been fulfilling, it surely hasn't been easy; anything but. Living with a career like mine has unique challenges, but because it really is my "calling" God has given me and those around me the grace to do it. Money has not always flowed easily, and it's taken fifteen years to get to this point. If it were not for my wife and family supporting and encouraging me not to quit and our absolute belief that this is what God wants us to do, we never would have made it. God has provided for me in ways I never would have imagined, sometimes supernaturally, from sources I never would have planned on, that has allowed me to continue pursuing my assignment.

Another thing that is hard about me having this calling to write is it's so "out of the box" that a lot of people just don't get me. It's hard trying to explain to some more traditional or conventional people what you do for a living. But when I read the hundreds of letters I've received from readers saying how God used my writing to touch their lives it makes it all worth it. Letters like these:

"I loved your book. It made me feel that normal isn't that far away from me. It made me feel that I was worthy on a day when I just knew I was completely worthless. On that day outside that coffee shop I opened your book and let the tears dry naturally, and began to read, and today, two days later, I don't feel alone and hopeless. I feel a deep sense of trust, like a child. Thank you. God bless you."
                                                        —Anna, Florida

"Your book has inspired me to step off the plank and pursue my dreams . . . I thought I was a failure but then you reminded me to enjoy the journey. I am going to trust God to get me there. Please continue to write. Your outlook on life is wonderful."

—Robin, Philadelphia, PA

Finally, I would like to say that hitting rock bottom knocked me out of my comfort zone and forced me to deal with issues in my life that were being swept under the rug and were holding me back from being all I could be. It also put me in a position to try for something I may have never tried otherwise. A friend of mine once said, "Hitting rock bottom can be a good thing because it gives you something to push off of." Remember, when you are in the dark pit and it seems like you will never get out, don't give up. Don't give in to despair. God knows where you are. Cry out to Him and He will bring you out to something new and better than ever before.

Max Davis has authored sixteen books, including ten collaborations. His work has been featured in *USA Today,* on the *Today Show,* and the *700 Club.* To learn more about Max's past books and upcoming projects, visit www.maxdavisbooks.com.

Victories

◆

Peggy Fleming—Olympic Gold Medalist, Cancer Survivor, and Entrepreneur

"If we all did the things we are capable of doing,
we would literally astound ourselves."

—Thomas A. Edison

I grew up in San Jose, California. My parents encouraged my three sisters and me to try different kinds of activities. With four girls in the family, there were many afternoons devoted to dance classes, softball games, art, and, of course, ice skating. Each one of us found what we liked and followed it. For me, it was skating. As a kid, it came natural to me. I stepped out onto the ice at age nine and thought, "Wow, this is easy!" It was fun, and I was good at it. The ice was so smooth and the air was crisp. I even loved the sound of the skate gliding across the ice. I kept stepping onto the ice and got better and better. There was a spark, the kind that kids have when they have a natural ability. The spark goes off and everything just progresses. I loved it.

Though we weren't wealthy by any means, I was able to take some private lessons. After about a year of lessons with my first coach, we realized that I could actually go somewhere with skating. We got serious. I started competing and won my first competition. Everything clicked. But, of course, life isn't always like that. In the next competition I came in dead last. As a kid, though, I wasn't really upset. I guess I didn't really have the competitive spirit yet. Here it was, my first month of competitive skating, and I had already experienced the thrill of victory and the agony of defeat. That's when my competitive spirit began. I was doing something I was pretty good at, but now, if I wanted to keep skating, I had to pay attention. Simply expecting everything to just "click" wasn't going to cut it.

Once I got more serious about competing, I focused my mind on being my best. I learned that you have to take everything one step at a time. I wanted to win every practice session. Every lesson. I wanted everyone to recognize my ability. Things were going well.

Then, in 1961, the unthinkable happened. My coach Bill Kipp and the top American ice skaters and coaches were on their way to the World Figure Skating Championships. They were killed in a plane crash. It was devastating. It was such a deep tragedy to the sport of figure skating. My family and I were shocked. The world was shocked. All of the major American skaters were gone. My coach was gone. I knew that something big had happened, but again, I was only twelve years old. I don't think I felt the full impact that this event would have on our entire sport.

My mom was great at handling everything. She helped me to stay positive and focused, and she made sure I was dealing with everything on a daily basis. Her support really helped me cope. She was at every practice and made sure I was progressing. And, if she didn't think it was working, we changed coaches. I wound up changing coaches several times over the years. Now, as an adult, I understand and appreciate the effort she put into my success. As a kid, I didn't realize how much she made a difference. She took things one step at a time. Though the financial pressure may have affected the family, she never let me know it. If she saw we needed a change, she simply said, "Well, we need a change," and she made it happen.

I kept skating. At fifteen I made the 1964 Olympic Team in Innsbruck, Austria. It was an incredible experience and very eye-opening. I was a pretty shy girl, so the caliber of the competition was a bit intimidating. But I just went with the flow and did one competition at a time. When you skate the same routine over and over it becomes muscle memory, so I just went out there and did what I had been practicing. I wound up placing sixth in my first international competition. In some ways, I still can't believe I did it. That first Olympics was like being in a dream.

Four years later when I competed in the 1968 Olympics, I entered as the two-time World Figure Skating Champion. I felt the pressure. Everyone was out to beat me. I just wanted to beat myself and be better than last year. It worked. My goal, my dream of the gold medal, was finally a reality.

Most remarkable, 1968 was the first time the Olympic Games were televised live and in color. After that, so much happened, so fast. My life became a bit more, well, glamorous. My first professional job was starring in a one-hour television special on NBC. There were endorsements, photo shoots, the Ice Follies, and more television specials. My life and success fell into place.

Flash forward to 1998. I was commentating and performing, and everything was going well. Life was good, as they say. I was at the U.S. Figure Skating Championships in Philadelphia—the same place I won before going to the 1968 Olympics. The entire 1968 figure-skating team gathered for this event. We all skated around the ice. Earlier in the evening, I was getting dressed. I was stretching and trying to relax. Suddenly I noticed something. I saw this lump on my chest. *Huh,* I thought. *Maybe it's just a pulled muscle.* There wasn't a lump on the other side, so I thought I must have really pulled something. I didn't think it was anything serious because I had just had a mammogram and a checkup five months earlier.

After the championships, I kept working for the next two weeks, but the lump was still there. To ease my mind, I scheduled a doctor's appointment. After a couple appointments, a needle biopsy, and a surgical biopsy, I heard the news. It wasn't good. I was diagnosed with breast cancer. It was shocking. I thought, *I'm a healthy athlete. I'm in great shape. Never missed a doctor's appointment. How could I have cancer?* It was so unexpected. There I was—life was going well. Needless to say, my life as I knew it came to a screeching halt.

In a weird way, it was much like when I came in dead last after winning my first competition. I was used to winning, and this felt like a loss. It just shook me. I had always had good checkups, so I took my good health for granted. The whole thing was a huge surprise. The only injuries I'd ever had were from accidentally tripping over something. I think my background in skating helped me cope. You don't win the Olympics overnight, and you don't recover from cancer overnight. I took it one step at a time.

My friends and family gave me amazing support. Part of defeating cancer is maintaining a positive attitude. My husband, Greg, my friends, and my doctors all told me that I would survive. Believing in them helped me to believe in myself. It helped me stay positive. I decided that I wanted to come back strong and still be myself. I was not going to go down the path of feeling sorry for myself, so I committed to doing everything the doctors told me to do. I never missed an appointment. I exercised. Since I was already in pretty good shape, I did some weight training, but I worked out a little lighter. I ran with a couple of friends. They always kept me on track, even though we ran a bit slower. They were always there for me.

Just like when my mom managed my coaches, my friends and family kept my spirit alive, making sure I was progressing to the best of my ability. They encouraged me and kept me focused on getting better. In a way, fighting cancer was like skating practice. In order to win, or in this case beat breast cancer, I had to pick myself up, have confidence in myself, and stay focused on the goal.

♦ ♦ ♦ ♦

After all the hard work, the tears, and the constant attempts
to tell my fear to go away, I survived. The cancer was gone. From
family, to friends, to doctors, even strangers, I'll never, ever forget the love and support I received. My diagnosis, although challenging me and shaking me to my core, helped me move on with
life. My past accomplishments are part of who I am, but I have
enjoyed moving forward. And, after surviving cancer, I won't let
anything pass me up.

In 1999, my husband Greg and I had an inspiration. We
decide to plant Chardonnay vines on our property in Los Gatos,
California. Making wine was not our original intention. We
simply planted some vines for a landscaping project. Planting
vines was relatively inexpensive and they were really beautiful,
so we thought it'd be a great idea. We started selling our
Chardonnay grapes to another winery, but our grapes made
up only 1 percent of the grapes they were using in their wine.
We were disappointed because we couldn't taste our grapes in
the wine. We thought, *Maybe we should bottle our own!* So we
gave it a shot. And you know what? It was pretty good! We
just went with the flow, kind of like when I was skating.
Things just progressed.

In 2003, Greg and I established our bonded winery. Hence,
Fleming Jenkins Vineyards & Winery was born. We had always
loved good food and good wine, so it was an amazing feeling to
bottle our own wine, especially from what had started out as our

little landscaping project! Now Greg and I are farmers, and we have a tasting room on Main Street in Los Gatos. Our operation is fairly small; we make all of our wine in town at the historic Novitiate Winery and have become part of the history of a winery that's been active for more than a hundred years.

This new chapter of our lives has opened up so many opportunities. One of the most gratifying is our wine named Victories, which we started producing in 2004. It's a dry rosé made from a Pinot Noir and a touch of Syrah. We chose rosé because its pink color reminds us of the pink color that symbolizes the campaign against breast cancer. We donate approximately two dollars of every bottle we sell to breast cancer research, awareness, and outreach. So far, we've donated more than $30,000 with our Victories campaign. This wine is also a reminder to me about the many victories in my life, from the Olympics, to beating breast cancer, and more. The statement on the back label of the wine bottle sums it up, "Victories is a wine created for the celebration of the personal accomplishments, large and small, that unite us, sustain us, and inspire us every day." Hopefully, someday soon, we'll all celebrate a victory over breast cancer by finding a cure.

Victories was recently voted one the best rosés in the country. A victory indeed! It goes to show that when you set out to do something, no matter what it is, you have to stay positive. You've got to think, *I can do this.* It's an energy that comes from within that makes things happen. If you go into something thinking, *Oh, God, I hope I can do this,* well, it's not going to be that same energy. It's like when you compete and after they call your name, you skate out to the middle of the ice rink to take your spot. You can't go out there with the attitude, "I hope I don't fall." You have to go out there thinking, *I'm prepared. I want to do this. I want to show you what I can do.*

Earlier in life I never, ever thought I would have a winery. Since being diagnosed with cancer, I've relearned to do what makes me happy—to keep growing in new areas. The act of reinvention has been wonderful for both me and my husband. We are doing something we love because we weren't afraid to try. You know, I've even started painting in the last five years. I was so nervous at first, afraid of the canvas. It would take me weeks, months even, to finish a painting. I heard an art teacher say something that changed my perspective on painting. He said, "Don't be afraid of the canvas," and he would squirt paint all over it and say, "See, it's really easy." So when I approached my next painting, I thought, "Yes, that's not so hard!" Then I would just go with it, layering the paint on the canvas one stroke at a time.

It's all about layers when it comes to painting, and it's all about layers in life, too. That's what makes you who you are. Thinking about life in these terms has really changed my outlook. I am building on my layers. Being an Olympian is one of them—but not the only one. And now I've got the winery. Another layer. And I paint. Yet, another layer. Life is full of moments of reinvention. And, yes, victories are possible, they are obtainable, and a winning spirit will guide you in setting your goals and achieving them.

Peggy Fleming won an Olympic gold medal for figure skating in 1968 and has been a television commentator for the sport for more than twenty years. In 1993, an Associated Press survey ranked Fleming as the third most popular athlete in America, behind fellow Olympians Mary Lou Retton and Dorothy Hamill and ranking ahead of other major sports stars such as Michael Jordan, Joe Montana, and 800 other athletes. Fleming, a breast cancer survivor, and her husband now own and operate Fleming Jenkins Vineyards & Winery in California. A portion of wine sales goes to support breast cancer awareness. To learn more, visit www.flemingjenkins.com.

Never Call Him a Victim

◆

Bob Wieland—
The Most Courageous Man in America

"Everything can be taken from a man
but one thing: the last of the human freedoms—
to choose one's attitude in any given set of
circumstances, to choose one's own way."

—Viktor Frankl

Voted "The Most Courageous Man in America" by the National Football League Players Association, Bob Wieland had it all— looks, brains, athletic ability, and was well on his way to becoming a professional baseball player. In high school, in the 1960s, Bob was never a kid who wandered aimlessly around with no plans or goals. No, Bob Wieland had a dream and did everything in his power to make that dream come true.

His goal was to become a pitcher for the Philadelphia Phillies or New York Mets. That dream may sound too grand for many, but not to Bob. To prepare for the love of his life, baseball, he practiced relentlessly, dedicating himself above and beyond all the other athletes around him. Eventually, his perseverance and hard work paid off. He became an all-star. Then, when he pitched a complete game with a total of nineteen strikeouts, which broke a high school league record, scouts from the Philadelphia Phillies expressed an interest in signing him to a contract. Bob's dream was actually coming true and he was elated! Life could not have been better. About that same time, however, he received another offer that he couldn't refuse. It was a draft notice from Uncle Sam's team calling him to the Vietnam War.

Disappointed, but proud to serve his country, Bob thought that he'd be home within a couple years to play professional baseball. The Phillies had agreed to wait for him. With that assurance, he dreamed of the day his family would meet him at the airport waiting to cheer him home. On June 14, 1969, however, his dreams were forever altered when he stepped on a booby-trapped 82-millimeter mortar while attempting to rescue a fellow soldier.

Bob says, "I remember when the moment of truth first dawned on me. [In the hospital] I glanced down at the white sheet and slid my hands cautiously down to touch my legs. There was nothing there. Pulling the sheet to one side, I looked down and saw huge bandages wrapping my upper thighs and the long, bare expanse of white sheet . . . Later I was told that the mortar I'd stepped on had blown my legs in one direction, my body in the other. Half of my blood had poured into the earth like rain.

I was on the final countdown when an unidentified soldier from my company got me to a helicopter that had been rerouted at the last moment. I was alive—though no longer six feet tall and weighing 205 pounds. I was two feet, ten-and-a-half inches tall, weighing 87 pounds."[3]

The next several months proved to be the toughest on Bob as he stayed in the hospital for rehab and physical therapy. One morning he woke early with a new throbbing, relentless pain in his "stumps" as he calls them. The doctor said it was a sign that he was beginning to heal. But along with the healing pain came a new wave of anguish that flooded him to the depths. At twenty-two, was his life as an athlete really over? The question haunted him, and the obvious answer was "yes." He had no legs. What kind of athlete could he be? Yet, in his spirit, Bob Wieland refused to give in to despair or play the role of victim.

"I knew what 'seems to be' and what 'is' are two different things. As I lay in that hospital and stared at the ceiling day after day I determined that my dream was not going to end just because I had no legs. So I had to overcome an obstacle? I'd done it before. I could do it again. I promised myself one thing: with God's help, I could and would overcome all obstacles. In my heart and soul I was an athlete. Surely there was a sport out there I could compete in. It was obvious by the way doctors and nurses treated me that they thought of me as 'handicapped.' So, almost

---

[3] Bob Wieland, *One Step at a Time: The Remarkable True Story of Bob Wieland* (Grand Rapids, MI: Zondervan, 1989), 23.

in spite of them, I determined to think of myself as an able-bodied individual. When I thought I was strong enough to get out of bed, I convinced the doctors and nurses to take me outside for some fresh air. I'll admit that it took me forty-five minutes to get out of bed and into the wheelchair, and each move I made increased the excruciating pain. But I did it. A nurse wheeled me out into the hot summer air. Though oppressive, it was delightful. I took three breaths of it and fell asleep, exhausted. When I woke up I was back in bed. So much for my first outing."[4]

After arriving back in the states, even though Bob tried to stay optimistic, he fell into a deep depression as day after day he sat in his wheelchair, bored, thinking about the severity of his handicap, his immense limitations, and the life he once had. The victim mentality and self-pity started to creep over him again. How *does* one handle going from a star athlete to a double amputee? One can't begin to imagine the pain and frustration of wanting so desperately to get up, to walk, to run, to drive to the store, but not being able to do so. Bob eventually came to the somber realization that he *must* do something. True, his body was broken and he couldn't do certain things; still, he could not let his life just waste away before his eyes. Something drastic needed to happen. He had to reinvent himself in a completely new way. Bob Weiland desperately needed a do over. But how? Was it even possible?

With all the mental strength he could muster, Bob once again rejected the victim mentality and dug deep down in his soul for

---

[4] Ibid., 25.

courage. It was that same courage he drew from to rescue his fellow soldier, and somewhere in his core he found it—the courage to do whatever it took to get his life back—to reinvent himself. Then, after contemplating his available resources, his options, and crying out to God, Bob got an inspired idea. "I may not have my legs, but I still have what's really important. I have my mind, my spirit, my hands, and my connection with my Creator. I can become a model of possibility for other Vietnam vets. I'm going to walk across the United States on my hands!"

Of course, Bob had his share of critics and naysayers. "Walk across the United States on your hands? Are you crazy? Your depression is causing you to think unrealistically." Others simply raised their eyebrows in doubt. "Look, I feel for you. I'm sorry for your disability, but come on, be sensible. Nobody can walk across the country on their hands." Nevertheless, on September 8, 1982, Bob took the first step of his journey at Knott's Berry Farm in Orange County, California. He finished in Washington, D.C., on May 14, 1986—a journey of four years, eight months, and six days; 2,784 miles; and 4,900,016 steps. His quest ended at the Vietnam Memorial, panel 22W, line 47. Carved into the black granite on line 47 was the name *Jerome Lubeno*, the man Bob was trying to rescue when he stepped on the mortar.

Bob's heroic journey was a defining moment, a turning point. It was a dramatic event that began his total life reinvention, and he would never be the same. Afterward, he went on to break the world record in the bench press for his weight class and to compete in several marathons in his wheelchair. Bob became the strength and motivational coach for the Green Bay Packers football team and was the only double amputee to compete in the grueling Ironman Triathlon in Kona, Hawaii. He has helped raise millions of dollars for worthy projects such as Food for the Hungry International. But perhaps Bob's greatest achievement is his ability to encourage others, which he does at high school and elementary school assemblies everywhere.

Today, Bob is happily married and continues to be a shining example for others around the world. If he can take his broken body and reinvent himself in such a powerful way, surely we can too! Like Bob, let us throw off our excuses, let go of the victim mentality, and do whatever it takes to reinvent ourselves.

Bob Wieland is a powerful inspirational and motivational speaker. To learn more about Bob check out www.bobwieland.com.

Sources

Wieland, Bob. *One Step at a Time: The Remarkable True Story of Bob Wieland.* Grand Rapids, MI: Zondervan Books, 1989.

http://www.fivestarspeakers.com/espeakers/3270/BobWieland.html.

http://www.montgomerynews.com/articles/2010/02/07/north_penn_life/sports/doc4b6c62e32fd74169449632.txt.

One Act of Courage,
a Whole New Life Path

◆

Jim Eschrich—Author, Speaker,
and Personal Dream Maker

"Only by attempting the absurd can we
achieve the impossible."

—Anonymous

I couldn't believe I was actually in Winterberg, Germany, for a whole month, nestled in the countryside north of the Alps as a member of the U.S. Bobsled Team. It was surreal being there, but it was even more surreal how I got there. I tried out for the team, even though I had never bobsledded before in my life. In fact, I was petrified of roller coasters. For those of you who may not know, bobsledding is much more dangerous than roller coasters. A roller coaster only gives the illusion of risk. It's only an illusion because roller coasters actually ride on safety rails. In bobsledding, while there is a track with lips to confine the carnage in the event of a crash, there are no safety rails. You and your team take on all the responsibility and all the risk. There's one for you—a guy petrified of roller coasters on the U.S. Bobsled Team!

The flight over to Germany had given me plenty of time to ponder the incredible new path my life was now on. I thought about all those people who told me I'd never make it, that I was crazy to think I could pull it off, that I was just wasting my time even thinking about it. Don't get me wrong; my critics had a good case. I mean, who in their right mind tries out for the U.S. Bobsled Team at age thirty? Maybe it would have made sense if I'd been a trained athlete with years of experience who knew what he was doing. But I wasn't any of those things. In high school I played one sport—football—and sat on the bench most of the time, especially after being diagnosed with Crohn's disease—an inflammatory bowel disorder. Then, my knee got torn up in college during a pickup game of touch football. Years later that same injury led to my medical discharge from the United States Marine Corps Officer Candidates School. I liked lifting weights, but that's a far cry from being an athlete. Nope, there wasn't anything spectacular about my athletic background. My bobsled teammates, well, that was an entirely different matter. Many were highly trained college football players and track athletes.

Two years earlier I'd been lying in bed staring up at the ceiling, terrified—terrified of where my life was and terrified of where it was going. At almost thirty years old, I was unmarried, with no prospects and no sense of direction. Most of my friends had families and were settled into their careers. They were doing the safe and expected things. I was trying my hand at safe and expected, but wasn't having much luck.

I knew lying there that somehow, some way, I had to take my life in a different direction. I wanted to feel passionate about something, anything, but what? I needed a passionate do over. Then, an idea popped into my mind. I remembered hearing Jim McKay's voice broadcasting from the Lake Placid Winter Olympic games and on ABC's *Wide World of Sports* when his voice would boom those famous words, "The thrill of victory and the agony of defeat."

Lake Placid was only a few hours away from where I was living at the time, and I got to thinking about the bobsled races that had been broadcast from there. Even though I'd never done it, I'd always been intrigued by bobsledding. My first memory of the sport goes all the way back to the 1968 Winter Olympics in Grenoble, France. *You should try out for the bobsled team,* I thought to myself. As crazy as the idea sounded, the thought persisted in my mind, and after letting the dream cultivate for a while, I decided to go for it.

Nearly everyone thought I was crazy when I told them I was trying out for the bobsled team. Sure, I'd get comments like, "That's nice, keep me posted." But it sounded an lot awful like, "We don't have any open positions right now, but we'll keep your résumé on file." Nobody was taking me seriously. One friend of mine, a sensible-type guy, told me point-blank that I needed to grow up, that I didn't have a chance athletically, and that I'd be competing against highly trained Olympic athletes.

He was right in that it certainly appeared I didn't have a snow-ball's chance of succeeding, but, hey, what did I have to lose? My sensible friend now has a framed, autographed picture of me taken at the U.S. Olympic bobsled trials hanging in his office!

Trying out for the bobsledding team and making it proved to be a pivotal point in my life. My entire attitude about myself and how I would move forward in the future changed. It took me off the path of conformity and put me on a path of originality, passion, and courage. The nature of the challenge was exactly what I needed at the time.

My story is about ordinary people like you and me being capable of doing extraordinary things when we tap into our core passions. The term *courage* is derived from the Latin root *cor*, which literally means *heart* or *core*. The original use of the word *courage* meant to *stand by one's core*. Standing by one's core *is* living authentically, or living true to our core self. It's here, in our center, that true passion resides.

For me, the prospect of sitting behind a desk for the rest of my life was about as passionless of an existence as I could have imagined for myself. Yet, there I was just going through the motions of life while my core self, the authentic me, was slowly but surely wasting away. To live passionately, I decided a revolution was in order, and since bobsledding was the only thing on my radar that was giving me goose bumps, bobsledding it was. Trying out for the team seemed simple enough. All I had to do was go to Lake Placid, take an eight-event test, pass it, and I would be on the U.S. Bobsled Team. The test consisted of 30-,

60-, 100-, and 300-meter sprints; five consecutive hops for distance; a vertical jump; throwing a sixteen-pound shot from between your knees; and cleaning a weight from the floor to your shoulders. Obviously, the faster you ran, the greater the distance you hopped, the further you threw the shot, and so on, the more points you were awarded. The objective was to see how explosive you were, which was an important trait given the fact that you'd be pushing a several-hundred-pound sled from a dead stop.

The first time I tried out I failed miserably, falling hundreds of points short of the 650-point minimum required. I was so bad, it was embarrassing. It was at this point I think I officially hit bottom. *Maybe all those naysayers are right,* I thought. *Maybe it's crazy to think I can do this.* But one thing I've learned is, if there's a blessing in hitting bottom, it's that you finally have something to push off of. It was either push off or stay defeated on the bottom. Fortunately, I chose the former and decided to give it another shot, only this time I was determined to learn from my past failures and prepare myself like never before. I trained hard and I trained smart. I sprinted. I lifted. I found myself a track and weight-lifting coach. I practiced the events contained in the test and even hired a sports psychologist to help wring out of me the last few drops of whatever potential I had. No stone was left unturned. Coming back to Lake Placid the second time around I was well prepared and confident. And two days after the testing began, the results were in. I had made the team by a whopping one point! That's right, one single point.

Still, I had shown great improvement, and regardless of how close it was, I had made the U.S. Bobsled Team.

After my time on the team, I was a changed man. You can't come out of nowhere to make the national bobsled team, go to the Olympic trials, and not have it leave an indelible mark on you. Dramatic and intense experiences are like that. I had made a dream become a reality. Now, instead of having feelings of trepidation, I soared with confidence. What other dreams could I make come true? I didn't know the answer, but I couldn't wait to find out.

I never went back to living that old, safe, and predictable life. I became a single-engine flight instructor and commercial-rated glider pilot. These had been childhood dreams of mine. I became an entrepreneur, opening my own home-based market research business. This, in turn, allowed me to be more available to my two girls after experiencing a divorce. I got into real estate, purchasing duplexes. I took up karate in my forties, eventually becoming a brown belt, and then took up snowboarding. And I've done other things that inspired me, including becoming scuba qualified, a certified personal trainer, and running with the bulls in Pamplona, Spain . . . twice! Basically, thanks to my bobsled experience, I became my own little dream maker. Hands down, the best of my experiences is the one that gave me the courage to strike out on my own in business, which in turn allowed me to be there for my girls.

Prior to bobsledding I had lived much of my adult life in black and white, anchored to others' expectations of me. It wasn't until years later, until that morning in Syracuse, New York, when I woke up thinking about what a disappointment my life had been, that I said, *"Screw this!"* Conforming or fitting in wasn't cutting it for me. So I pulled anchor and dropped it dead center on the sport of bobsledding. I gave myself permission to have a do over. For one year I lived as passionately as I ever had. I felt truly alive. Everything I did had a purpose. Nothing was taken for granted. And living this way, just once, changed me forever. From then on, I was committed to living passionately. Sure, it takes some courage to live this way, but not as much as you might think. When your passion is engaged, you're not preoccupied with the danger, the fear, or the pain, but you're focused on the destination, the goal. Everything else becomes a sideshow.

Passion, and far less so, courage, is at the core of a well-lived life. And our passions run no deeper than when it comes to our children. While going through a divorce several years ago I was deeply concerned what it would do to them. They didn't have any say in the events that were forced upon them. Would their self-esteem plummet? Would their grades suffer? Would they withdraw? Would they grow up afraid of commitment? And how would I get along with my ex-wife? What kind of example would we set for our children? And how would I behave as a single guy with two kids? Scary questions. And even scarier answers if you don't have a belief system that you feel passionate about. No, I'm not drifting into a long-winded religious discussion. That's not me. My kids are my passion. This is something my ex-wife and I will always share. We may disagree, and God knows we can aggravate the hell out of each other, but at the end of the day we're both committed to doing what's right for the kids. Because of our passion for our children, we get along remarkably well. I never, and I repeat, never would have thought it possible. Yet, it's not unusual for one of us to be at the other's house helping out with homework or something that the girls are going through. Is it always easy and carefree? Hello, we're divorced. But if getting along together is better for our girls, if it steadies them while everything else in their world is changing, well, it's worth it. We do whatever it takes. Platitudes about courage do not make you courageous. What you passionately believe in does. Find things to believe in. Take them to heart and let no one or anything tread on them.

Reinventing your life in whatever direction you desire requires passion and courage. It also takes stepping outside your comfort zone and taking action. Face it, there are a lot of things that we want to experience in life, but few of us are willing to actually take the steps to turn them into reality. We are hesitant to give ourselves permission for a do over. Instead, we tend to have this "I'm along for the ride" mentality, as if we have no real choice in the matters of life. As a result, we let the ride of life take us where *it* would have us to go. Well, at some point, we must pull ourselves out of the backseat, grab ahold of the wheel, and take control.

Let's take this present economy, for example. None of us have a crystal ball that will give us a clear vision of the future. If we did, we wouldn't be in this mess to start with. The best way to determine your future is to take charge of creating it. Take some personal responsibility. Grab the wheel and get moving! Roll up your sleeves, let your inner passion and what matters most to you be your road map, and get to work on your dreams.

When we recognize our ability to make choices, then difficulties, like the economy, can offer many great opportunities for those individuals who are alert, who are willing to be flexible and take calculated risks, and are not afraid to work. Even when we hit bottom, and I've been there, we still have a choice. We can hit bottom and stay there, or we can use the bottom to push off of and struggle back to the surface. Remember this: whenever we are frustrated or confronted with a deep dilemma, there's usually a hidden opportunity waiting to be uncovered and acted on.

Sometimes it's necessary to manufacture the dramatic and create your own do over in order for real change to occur. For me, it began with my trying out for the bobsled team. When you look at others who've experienced an unusual degree of success, quite often they created it by attempting the dramatic. In other words, most people would have called them crazy for pursuing a pipe dream. But by not minding what naysayers said, they were driven by their passion and refused to be dissuaded.

Jim Eschrich lives in Lenexa, Kansas, a suburb of Kansas City. He's a dynamic speaker and author on the subject of passion-inspired courage. For information about Jim and his book, *Courage for the Rest of Us: Going from Ordinary to Extraordinary*, go to his website at www.courage4us.com or e-mail him at jim@courage4us.com.

Those Two Boys

◆

Michael Trufant—Author, Leadership Coach/
Business Consultant, and Cancer Survivor

"The robb'd that smiles steals something from the thief."

—William Shakespeare

I've always been a high-energy, driven, bottom-line kind of guy. For thirteen years, I was president of a wireless company and lead the team that grew it from almost nothing to more than $20 million in annual revenue. I've taken over multiple businesses and started several, including a dot-com that was successfully acquired. I'm a person that sees possibilities and attracts people to opportunity. If I feel passionate about a project, I love to pull them in. To me, it's dishonorable to pull people into something that is ultimately not in their best interest. But when I see projects, start-ups, services, anything that I believe makes sense and can make a genuine contribution to those I'm influencing, then it's a great win. And that's inspiring to me. That's been the magic of my life.

In 1999, at the age of forty, I felt like Mr. Invincible, moving and grooving, slaying dragons and making money in the process, when I found a bump on my neck. Because I was blowing and going, I didn't think too much about it. My wife, however, insisted that I get it looked at. So I went in and the doctor did a biopsy. When I didn't get a call back for a couple weeks I figured there was nothing to it, no big deal. Sure enough, a few weeks later, I was at work and got a call at about 3:00 in the afternoon. It was the doctor's office: "We have your pathology reports and we'd like to give them to you," the caller said.

"Fine, just tell me," I replied.

"Well, we'd like you to come in," was the response.

"Just tell me," I insisted. "I've got a lot going on and I won't be available until five-thirty or six o'clock."

"That's alright. We'll be here."

I agreed to stop by later that afternoon. I knew something must be up, but had no clue as to how serious it was. It had been out of my mind, and during those few weeks of waiting, I had resigned from one company, started another, got involved with another, celebrated my fortieth birthday, and had my tenth wedding anniversary.

When I walked into the doctor's office, the nurse followed me in. I knew for sure now that something was going on. After I sat down, the doctor said, "I have your report."

"Let me guess—cancer?" I said, kind of joking.

He said, "Yeah."

"Okay. Tell me more."

"Desmoplastic neurotropic melanoma."

"What's that?" I asked.

"I don't know exactly. It's melanoma. It's rare, and it took us three weeks to get the diagnosis back."

At this point I was in flat denial. "Okay," I said. "What do we do? How do we fix it? What's the procedure?"

"I'm going to get on a conference call tomorrow and find out all about it," he said. "We'll have to set up surgery."

I didn't respond and sat there for a moment processing all of what he'd just said. I thought, *All right, surgery. I can handle that. Scrape it out or whatever and I'm back in business.* The seriousness hadn't hit me.

"Are you okay?" he asked.

"Yeah, I'm great." Like I said, I was in denial. I didn't have enough information to panic or not. I had never been confronted with that kind of diagnosis or that kind of thing.

I called a friend whose brother is one of the nation's top pathologists and told her I'd been diagnosed with desmoplastic neurotropic melanoma. Later, after talking to her brother, she called me back. "You got a minute?" she asked.

"Sure."

"You might want to sit down," she said.

"Okay, I'm sitting."

"You have a very rare, very dangerous, and very destructive cancer. It's not good, Michael."

I remember feeling like I'd been shot. I mean, you wake up one day and your sky is blue, then you get this news and suddenly

your sky is black—dark, stormy black. It all started to hit me as
I moved from denial to fear. I like to be in control and I was not
in control. I was mad and frustrated. *What do we have to do to fix
this?* I kept asking myself. *I just want to fix this and get back in
the race.*

I called together my YPO (Young Presidents' Organization)
forum, a small local subgroup of CEOs that I meet with every
month for fellowship and to support one another. We all gathered and I told them the news. It just so happened that one of
the men in the group knew a top doctor at MD Anderson
Cancer Center. He picked up the phone and started calling him
right there. While he was making the call and all these CEOs
who care deeply about me were making their suggestions for
what I should do, at that moment, with the group around me, I
just zoned out and started thinking about my family. I almost
lost it. My two boys, Cade and Chris, then ages three and six,
came up in my mind. My whole world went away, and all I saw
were those two boys. At the end of the day, if it had been my
time to go, I'd have been fine. My wife would have made it. But
those two boys, they needed me. I'm a tough guy. Don't cry. I
can handle dying. My boys, on the other hand, they can break
me into pieces to this day. I looked up at my friends gathered
around me and blurted out, "I need to be here for my boys.
Guys, we gotta figure this out."

I got in at MD Anderson, and for that I am very grateful, but
throughout the whole process I was like a deer in the headlights.
I was scared. After all the tests, x-rays, and CT scans, the doctor

said, "What you have is very rare and very aggressive. When we go after this, we have to be as aggressive as possible." Then he told me, "Go home and get your affairs in order, and in a week we're going to do surgery and then start aggressive radiation treatments. We're going to get through it. But go home and focus on what's important."

At that point I was thinking, *I'm going to die.* All the stories about what could happen were running through my mind. The next week I had the six-hour surgery. Then, I started the radiation treatments, which barbequed the side of my head and throat. I couldn't swallow or eat solids. That took me out of play for about six months.

During all that time the overwhelming emotions I felt revolved around my two boys and my attitude. One night, the boys and I went to see the Disney movie *Tarzan.* I was sitting in the movie with them and had a big bolster on my neck. I had been cut on, sliced on. I was all messed up. We were sitting there, and the theme song for the movie came on by Phil Collins, "You'll Be in My Heart," which I believe ultimately says that even if I go away, even if I'm not here, you'll be in my heart. I was crying like there was no tomorrow. Now, whenever I hear that song I just bawl.

The doctor told me that quite often the difference between patients with good attitudes and patients with bad attitudes is living and dying. So, I had to work on my attitude, but in reality I was decimated emotionally. I was done. What really pulled me through were those two boys. That was my reason for living and my reason for the fight.

I had started going back to church. That's something one does when death is looming around the corner. Before this I wasn't hugely spiritual. Dying just wasn't on my radar. One Sunday I was sitting in the back of church crying and saying to myself, "What do I need to do to get right with you, God?" I was thinking, *I really should have paid more attention. Do I have to give money? Do I have to give my time?* I felt like I was making a deal. While I was sitting there, for the first time in my life, I believe I heard the voice of God. From deep within my core a voice that I knew didn't come from me said, "Don't worry about it, Michael. When it's your time I'll call you." It was that simple, that clear, deep in my spirit, yet it was loud. Before this, I mean, I was freaking out, running numbers and spreadsheets and bugging my doctors about my chances. God just said, "When it's your time I'll call you." At that moment, I can't quite explain it, but a peace washed over me that I had never experienced. *When God wants me,* I thought, *He'll take me. And when I go I get to go to someplace wonderful. I get to see my dad. So don't worry about it.* I walked out of church with the feeling of doom lifted.

A couple weeks went by and God spoke to me again, and it was accompanied by the same sense of peace. This has only happened twice in my life. This inner voice said, "I'm not ready for you yet. You still have something yet to do. You have a purpose." After that, the anxiety left and I went back to living. But I went back to living in a different way, with a new perspective.

Prior to cancer I was a race car with a lot of stuff to do. Now, I had focus and vision, but it was on the important things.

Before I was a doer, climbing ladders and such. Now I'm climbing ladders, but I'm asking, "Are they leaning against the right walls?" Before I was busy and active and productive, but I didn't know why I was doing it. I was a taker; now I work to be a giver. In my personal relationships I want to be a giver of positive energy and life, not a zapper of energy. I want to influence people for the right things. Now I have an intestinal fortitude. Before I was shooting shots; now I'm focused on where those bullets are going. I'm not scared anymore. Fear went away.

I don't waste time. Life is too short, and I see that there is a cost to not taking risks. It's the cost of regret. And I don't have time for relationships that don't matter. I was brought back to family and those edifying relationships. Life is too precious to be brought down by negative, toxic, and draining relationships. I'm very focused on engaging with people who have depth. I seek out genuine, intimate, and authentic conversations about the topics of life. When daily crises and bumps in the road come up, I now think, *Hey, it ain't cancer.* People say, "This is awful. This is terrible." I say, "It ain't cancer." It happens all the time.

I was very much torn down by cancer and radiation. It caused depression, sadness, and every reason not to recover. What gets you to recover? For me, it was family, the boys, faith, and the opportunity to do incredible things. Why are we here? If you can get the right perspective, you see it's just a matter of choices. Acceptance is one thing, and then you choose to take action. When you accept what your life is, then you can consider possibilities. A lot of people get stuck. They resign and don't take action. Action is the outcome of the perspective. The perspective is being where you are in the present and then making decisions on what you are going to do. While I had this horrible cancer and was looking death in the eye, I still had a choice. The choice was to pick up, give it my best shot, or to give up and waste away.

What do you want? Do you want to be a victim? It's a choice. You can overcome anything. People who pull out of the dip, people who succeed, are those who have a mind-set of taking positive action. I could have let the anger obsess me, blamed, been resentful, and pitiful, but I accepted my situation and asked, "What do I do?" Quite honestly, I didn't like the picture of being a victim or being depressed the rest of my life, regardless of how many years or months I had left. What I got from this experience was a kick in the butt to go try stuff. Even though I'd been busy and successful in some people's eyes, I had still been living in my comfort zone. Cancer got me out of my comfort zone and to start thinking about the really important things in life that I wasn't doing but needed to. Whatever a person is going through—whether it's cancer, divorce, being laid off, bankruptcy, you name it—there's a point at where it's decision time. Humans are the only creatures that can have perspective and envision their future. We have the ability to say, "Okay. This has happened. It's real. It's painful. I'm forever changed because of it. I accept it. Now, what are my choices and possibilities?" There are people in wheelchairs that do incredible things. There are people in wheelchairs who give up.

After going through this journey and gaining perspective, at fifty-three, I think I have the most incredible part of my life ahead of me. My sky was blue, and then my sky was black, but what happens is one day you get a little bit of the blue back and each day the blue grows. At some point, though, the black is always there; it's off on the side and you don't focus on it. You focus on the blue.

Michael Trufant is president of Solo North, LLC, a business consulting and executive coaching firm. He has been CEO of start-ups and established organizations. Michael most enjoys public speaking and assisting companies (and people) find focus and direction. He is an author and a member of YPO-WPO (Young Presidents' Organization/World Presidents' Organization). To contact Michael, visit www.solonorth.com.

A Reinvention to Quack About

♦

Jeanne Bice—Entrepreneur, Author, and Motivator of Women

"Why not go out on a limb?
Isn't that where the fruit is?"

—Frank Scully

Life was a lot different in the 1950s. Back then, to be successful if you were a woman, you went to college and then married a rich guy. Well, I did both. I got educated in lower elementary teaching and speech/drama. Then, in 1959 I married the richest kid in Ripon, Wisconsin. I became a wealthy housewife and thought my life was just wrapped up in a pink bow. My husband's name was Arlow and he owned franchises that installed elevator music all over the country. He also owned an AM/FM radio station in Ripon. Because I had the gift of gab and was somewhat of a socialite in our little town of 7,000, I got to host a one-hour talk show on the radio. It was called *Let's Get Away From It All,* and after several years, I had a mailing list of 55,000

women. I would take craft and cooking classes because that's
what wealthy wives did. I'd make stuff and then go on the radio
and talk about it. I was the queen of the town. My life was perfect until one beautiful, sunshiny day in 1981, my husband got
up from the lunch table and said, "I love you, Jeanne. I'll see you
tonight," and literally dropped dead at my feet of a massive heart
attack. I was forty.

Here's the thing: I had never paid a bill. I mean, when I ran
out of money in my checking account, the bank called my husband and said "she's out of money" and he'd put it in. I didn't
know how to do anything. I had been very, very pampered. I did
what a good wife does, was very good at it, and loved my job.
Then, God decided to downsize me.

Luckily, I didn't have any babies. My son was in college and
my daughter was a junior in high school. If I had had babies, I
think I would have committed hara-kiri. I had tons of friends
who were there to support me, but when the funeral was over
and the dust settled, I didn't have a dime to my name. It was all
family money, and my children had inherited the trust funds.
My husband hadn't planned on dying then and had very little
life insurance. So, my kids got the trusts, and I had to grow up
and figure out how the hell to support us. I was never so scared
in my life, not knowing where I was going to go or what I was
going to do to get money.

Some time before my husband died, I had a friend who was
going through a divorce and knew she wasn't going to get anything from her husband. Because we were close friends and

because I was on the radio, she wanted me to go into business with her—to open a women's retail shop. I really didn't want to, but my husband said, "Why? You make all this stuff, talk about it, and then give it away. Why not sell it?" So my friend and I opened up a retail store called the Silent Woman. We named it that because when women shop it's about the only time they're quiet. The store sold clothes, but also craft items, needlepoint, and my one-of-a-kind creations.

After my husband died, all I had was this retail business, but it wasn't making any money. The store had been a toy, a rich woman's toy. Now, my partner and I had to figure out how to make it work. We had leased a second store in Florida and wound up moving down there. My parents lived in Fort Lauderdale and I wanted to be close to them. Plus, my friend wanted to get out of the area. So, we shut down the store in Wisconsin and focused solely on the Florida store. It was a preppy clothing store and needlepoint shop. After a while, my partner got remarried and moved on with her life, leaving me to run the business alone.

Over the years I experienced one failure after another but somehow managed to stay afloat. The store began to evolve into a particular niche. Women would come into the store and they didn't want to just do needlepoint. They wanted to do needlepoint that they could put onto clothing. That's how I got into the appliqué business. Appliqué is a needlework technique where pieces of fabric or embroidery are sewn onto another piece of fabric to create designs, patterns, or pictures. I can't sew a stitch and can barely sew on a button, but in my lifetime I have trained hundreds of women how to appliqué just by talking and instilling in them the belief they could do it.

I was now seeing some success and caught the attention of a couple of businessmen who convinced me they could take the shop to another level. We partnered and expanded by opening a factory and were extremely successful, or so I thought. One day one of them walked into my office and said, "We can't make payroll."

"What do you mean we can't make payroll?"

"There's no money," he said.

When I tried to get the books to check them, they were nowhere to be found. I had trusted them and didn't pay attention. You can't do that. That's something I learned. Open every bill. Sign every check. Do not have a stamp. Without a stamp they can't rob you blind, but if you give them a stamp of your signature they can walk over you. I learned that lesson. It was a hard lesson to swallow because I lost what little savings I had put together to go into this business and had to start over from scratch. Yet, something inside refused to let me give up. I had a good support group of family and friends. I also leaned on God. I'm sorry, if you don't believe in God as a helper you *are* going to sink.

I took all the clothes that were left in the factory and started hand painting on them. I would paint all afternoon and into the night. Then, I took them to flea markets and they sold out. For about a four-year period I worked flea markets all over the country. I was about fifty years old and was hand painting

T-shirts and clothes sometimes nineteen hours a day. But it was never "woe is me." I just did what I had to do to survive. For me it was fear that I couldn't pay the rent. Do you know what it's like standing in the line at Sears to pay your light bill with a hundred other people, and you know they haven't got any money either? It doesn't do much for your self-esteem. But I never saw myself as a victim.

I learned another very big lesson. Don't ask God for just enough money to get by, because that's all you get. You'll get just enough to pay the bills before they turn it all off. Ask God for big stuff. One day a woman said to me, "Unless you believe you are worth it all, you'll only just get by." I would walk out of my house some days with money that I had found in the bottom of the couch or the bottom of a purse, and say over and over, "Thank you, God, I have more money than I will ever be able to spend in my lifetime." My brother was paying my rent. I had hit rock bottom! At fifty, I never thought I'd have money again. Now when people come up to me and say, "Oh my God, my husband was downsized. He's fifty years old and we're done!" I want to just shout at them and say, "Honey, I didn't get my dream until I was fifty. Don't cry about it. There are ways to make money. Just get off your fat ass and figure it out!"

For several more years I worked night and day selling clothes at flea markets and on street corners. I'd been engaged twice since I was widowed and luckily didn't marry again because they both died. I've buried three men and finally decided I'm past that point in my life and am not doing that anymore. My son,

Tim, who was helping in my business said to me, "You can't sell clothes on street corners the rest of your life; we've got to figure something out."

I just kept on making clothes and selling them, but every Monday morning we would have a meeting and Tim would say, "Well, Mom, have you figured it out yet?" and I would say, "Nope." But one day I walked into our Monday morning meeting and said, "I've found it. I know what I want to do. I saw this new show on cable. It's called QVC, and my mouth and I can do that."

I had a couple of sales reps who were trying to sell my clothes wholesale into stores and they said, "Oh, we can get you on QVC. No problem." But no rep could get us in. They just couldn't. Then, at one of our Monday meetings, Tim said to me, "Mom, you always say that your pastor preaches, 'If you can't do it, then give it to God.' Why don't we try giving it to God?" So we made a great big sign that read, "God-QVC-Yes," and we hung it on the wall in our office for everybody to see and then went about our business. Two weeks later the state of Florida called us and said they were calling young businesses in the state. They asked if we had ever heard of QVC—they were doing something called the 50/50 tour and were looking for new businesses. Would we like to try out?

I looked at my sign hanging on the wall and said, "Thank you, God." My daughter-in-law, Karin, and I drove to Orlando, just about three hours away, to the Tupperware Convention Center, and we unloaded a rolling rack with ten shirts on it from the car.

Other businesses were getting out of their vans with TVs and impressive presentations. We had ten shirts on a rolling rack. We rolled in and sat down at a table. The convention center was full of tables, each with businesses displaying their products. The evaluators went from table to table. They started evaluating at the table next to us and literally went all the way around the room in the opposite direction! We were the last table they visited that day. Many people had already left, and we figured they'd probably already made up their minds. I mean, we had ten shirts on a rack. But we said, "You know what? We've driven this far and we're hanging around." Well, we got picked. QVC picked twenty people from the state and we were number twenty-one. That meant we could only go if someone else dropped out. They did. This was the start of my tenth do over.

After the first show, QVC called us to come up to their studios in West Chester, Pennsylvania, outside Philly. I asked Tim if we didn't have a pot to pee in, how in the hell were we going to get to Pennsylvania? We had a few weeks, so he tended bar for a while to get some extra cash and I did some extra flea markets. We scraped together our money and drove to QVC. Let me tell you, it was worth the effort because we walked out of the building that first day with $350,000 worth of orders. We drove straight to the 7-Eleven to use the pay phone and called my daughter-in-law. I was excited, but also wondered where we were going to get the money to produce all the orders.

We'd never had to come up with that much in one fell swoop. We had to find a vendor that would work with us and went through a lot of "nos" until we finally hooked up with Elaine Lai in New York. The company made our goods for us. We now have many vendors. Elaine Lai is still one of them and is very important in our lives.

We figured out that we were really good at certain things. We are really good at selling, designing, and putting together a loyal following—just like I did back on the radio getting 55,000 women listeners in a very rural part of Wisconsin. We sucked at making clothes. So, Tim cut a deal with all these vendors, and now we do what we do well and they do what they do well and it's been a perfect merger. This year it will be sixteen years that we've been on QVC, and when we came the experts said we would never last.

When we first started at QVC our director said, "I'm getting rid of all the appliqué lines. We aren't going to do this anymore, but I can't get rid of you because you're part of the 50/50, and that's very important to us right now." He went on to say, "But I don't think you'll last six months because it's not upscale or chic enough." Well, we did last, ,and this not-upscale-enough line grew our business to more than $100 million.

When people say to me they can't find a job or they're too old to make a living, I have no tolerance for it. I worked really hard when I was poor. I worked eighteen to nineteen hours a day. People say, "Oh, you deserve your success, Jeanne. You worked really hard." I did work hard, but things really started to click once I gave it up and let God run that part of my life. I believe God puts a dream in every one of our hearts. I love selling clothes, but I really like motivating women to become more than they think they can be.

I'm only seventy and still believe I have a couple more do overs to come in my life. People think that the end of the world is coming; the sky is falling because the economy is going downhill. I live on a street in Boca Raton, and, honey, they're selling houses for $6 million and knocking them down to rebuild. Don't tell me the economy is falling out. There's money out there, and it's out there for the poorest of the poor and the wealthiest. There is enough money for everybody. There should be no poor. Many people are poor because they choose to be poor. The same is true for happiness. Happiness is a choice.

Some cry, "Oh, I don't have an education." That's poppycock. My education didn't have anything to do whatsoever with what I'm doing right now. I'm using my God-given talent, my mouth. My husband used to say I'm the only woman in the world with calluses on my ankle from putting my foot in my mouth so many times, but God gave me that mouth for a reason. It's a gift. The secret to real success and happiness is finding and using your gift. Who would have ever thought a fat kid from a farm in Wisconsin would make it in the fashion world . . . well, if I can do it, anyone can . . . go for the do over in your life.

Jeanne Bice is the creator of the famous Quacker Factory line of clothing. It is one of the most successful and sought after lines of clothing on QVC. Jeanne is also an author and motivator of women. You can find out more about her at www.quackerfactory.com.

Transformation

◆

Shannon Hammer—Motivational
Speaker and Author

"Never too late, never too old,
never too bad, never too sick,
to start from scratch,
and begin again."

—Yogi Bikram Choudhury

I remember the moment clearly. I was standing in a drugstore holding an envelope of pictures I had just developed. I pulled out a photo and saw an obese, young woman wearing a black party dress. Wait—I had a dress like that. Imagine my shock when a second later I realized that young woman was *me*. I hadn't recognized myself. What had happened to me? I was horrified.

Food: I'd come by my extra hundred pounds honestly. From childhood, I had deeply passionate, all-consuming love affair with food. I loved to eat. Nothing could get me out of bed like

the promise of pancakes dripping in butter and syrup. The antic-
ipation of the chocolate pudding cup waiting for me in my
lunch bag would distract me all morning. The best part about
visiting my grandparents wasn't the warm love I'd receive—it
was the spinach pies my grandmother would bake from scratch.

For obvious reasons, I developed a weight problem very early
in life. I personally wasn't conscious that I was overweight but
my girth did not go unnoticed by my family, where being thin
was an obsession.

A well-intentioned aunt put me on my first diet when I was
four. I remember not being allowed to eat the food I loved, like
potato chips and cupcakes, because they were "fattening."
Instead I was forced to eat "low-cal food" that I completely
hated—bitter grapefruit, runny yogurt, slimy celery.

I remember going with my family to restaurants and having
to order the popular restaurant staple at the time, the "Diet
Plate." When our food was served, I'd stare at the plates surrounding me that contained cheeseburgers and fries drenched in
chili, spaghetti and meatballs covered in sauce, and pot pies in
flaky pastry crusts. Then I'd look down at my own plate and see
the bunless, dry hamburger patty, a single scoop of cottage
cheese, and small bowl of syrupy peaches. I'd instantly feel
deprived, different, and discouraged.

Fat: Rather than help me lose weight, that diet set me up for
a binge-diet cycle that would last for the next thirty years of my
life. I spent the rest of my childhood completely obsessed with
both food and trying to lose weight.

My aunt was out of a job because by age six, I was putting myself on diets. I did whichever ones I could find, from Weight Watchers, to the Stewardess Diet (this was back when poor stewardesses were subjected to forced weigh-ins), to over-the-counter weight loss aids that promised to decrease hunger and render me immune to temptation.

I'd stick to each diet for a period of time, perhaps a week or two if I was lucky. The tension and hunger would build until I'd explode into a binge, shoveling food into my mouth with my fingers. It wasn't unusual for me to eat half a pan of leftover macaroni and cheese, a dozen slices of toast and butter, or a block of cheese and crackers in one sitting. If I had money, I'd ride my bike to the corner store and purchase an armload of Hostess products, which I'd devour and then hide the wrappers in my book bag, to be disposed of the next day at school. Must hide the evidence.

Despite my best efforts, by the time I was a teenager I carried an extra fifty to sixty pounds on my five-foot-six frame. I was deeply envious of the other normal-sized girls who I saw at school, wearing the clothes I wanted to wear, having the boyfriends I wanted to have. I hated my body with a passion and was deeply ashamed of how I looked. I hid under layers of mostly black clothes, baggy T-shirts and leggings, floor-length skirts, and long jackets that I refused to take off even in the hottest weather.

And still I dieted, and still I failed. This cycle continued throughout my twenties, only the diets got more expensive and the weight fluctuations more extreme. I developed a pattern of losing and gaining up to 100 pounds in a single year. My closet held a range of sizes from six to twenty. I had long since learned never to throw away my "fat clothes" because I knew I'd need them again soon.

Desperation: By my late twenties, I had moved from the hometown I'd lived in all my life and was living alone in a one-bedroom apartment. I was homesick, separated from family and friends, and felt trapped in a stressful job that I hated. I was desperately unhappy.

I stuffed down my feelings of loneliness and despair with food. Every night after work I'd sit in front of the television and devour entire bags of chips, half-gallons of ice-cream, boxes of cookies, and loaves of bread. I would eat until I was literally stuffed, and then I'd stagger into my bedroom and pass out. The next morning I would wake up with a stomachache and parched throat and vow that I was going to go on a diet. I'd swear to myself that I was going to the lose weight and this time—*this time*—I'd keep it off. And the next night, I would do the same thing again. I could not stop eating.

Denial is a very powerful thing. I saw the number on the bathroom scale. I knew that I weighed 100 pounds more than I should. I felt my ankles hurt as I walked across my small apartment. I saw the size-twenty jeans hanging in my closet that were now too tight. Perhaps it was because I had stopped looking at myself from the neck down, or perhaps reality was just too painful, but I didn't truly see how heavy I'd become until the day I saw that picture of me in that black dress.

Realizing the fat woman in the party dress was me broke through my denial. It woke me up. I knew I had to do something, but what? I'd done it all—I'd joined the gyms, popped the pills, mixed the powders, blended the shakes, paid the money, and none of it had worked. Ironically, that turned out to be the key to my eventual success.

Change: Sometimes you have to look at what doesn't work before you can see what does. I had a lifetime of failure—I had a vast arsenal of information on what didn't work. So now I could take that information and find out what did.

I knew I would have to completely revamp my way of looking at health, weight loss, and my body. I decided that no longer was I going to "go on a diet" with the intention of reaching a number on the scale and then going back to eating how I wanted. Rather, I was going to try to be *well*, not just *thin*, and seek health on all three levels—physical, emotional, and spiritual—for a lifetime.

Physical: Years of experience revealed that I was addicted to certain foods, just like an alcoholic is addicted to alcohol. Even though I could binge on anything in a pinch, I preferred to binge on refined carbohydrates and sugar. I realized I was going to have to give up my addictive substances, one day at a time, forever. I'd had a lifetime of being unable to control them, and I didn't see that changing any time in the near or distant future. The war was over—I lost.

I adopted a food plan that excluded my addictive food groups and also incorporated weighing and measuring to maintain portion control. In addition, I started writing down my food every day. That gave me the clarity and accountability that I needed to ensure I wouldn't slip into denial. In addition to my eating, I also revamped my exercise philosophy. My physical activity had pretty much followed the same all-or-nothing pattern as my eating—I was either aerobicizing every day or doing absolutely nothing.

Knowing how important exercise is to good health, I started out walking every day after work. At first I could only walk for twenty minutes before I had to head home, sweaty and exhausted. But before long, my legs grew stronger and I could go longer and faster. After a few months, to my surprise, walking was no longer challenging enough so I upgraded to exercise videos. Eventually I made my way back to the gym.

Emotional: All my life I had used food to cope. I ate when I was happy. I ate when I was sad. I ate to celebrate. I ate to console. I knew I was going to have to learn healthy ways of coping that didn't involve food. I joined a support group and made friends who advised and encouraged me. I learned to reach for the phone instead of food when I was unhappy. If I was stressed, rather than sit in front of the television with my hand in a bag of chips, I learned to write in my journal and "binge on paper." Slowly I replaced coping skills that did not work with ones that did.

Spiritual: When my unhealthy eating patterns disconnected me from my body, I also lost the connection with my inner voice, my intuitive self. Meditation became my ticket to reconnecting with my self. Knowing the power of meditation, I started to spend a few moments in the morning, breathing in and out, repeating a meaningful word to keep my mind occupied for several minutes. In addition to calming me, meditation also allowed me to access a vast well of inner strength and wisdom. As a result my stress levels decreased and my serenity increased.

Renewal: Over the course of three years, I lost 100 pounds. I've kept it off for more than seven years and my life has completely transformed. I went from barely being able to walk five minutes to now working out six days a week—five of which are done at 5:30 AM. I left the job I hated and went back to college, where I graduated with a 4.0 GPA, and started a career I loved and eventually married the man of my dreams.

My life may have completely transformed but one thing has remained the same—my wellness program. I still follow a personalized food plan, I still weigh, measure, and write down my food. I still get support, and I still meditate. Why? Because it still works and since it's not broken, I have no intention of fixing it.

And now I have the opportunity to help others. A few years ago, I got tired of writing down my food on scraps of paper and sticky notes. I also wanted to read something inspirational during my morning quiet time, so I went looking for a book that combined the two. As much as I looked, I couldn't find one—it didn't exist. So I figured I'd write it.

That book I couldn't find became my first published book, *The Positive Portions Food & Fitness Journal.* It's a six-month journal that I poured my years of experience, strength, and hope into to help others become their best selves.

Hope: I heard a woman say, "If there is breath in your body, there is hope." For many years, I thought there was no hope for me. I believed my destiny was to die obese and alone. I'm very happy to report that I was wrong—dead wrong.

When I started my journey to wellness, if I'd made a list of everything I wanted in life, I would have sold myself short. Today, I live a life beyond what I could have ever imagined for myself. I know that if this is true for me, it is equally true for you. If there is breath in your body, there is hope.

We can get a do over. Yes, indeed.

Shannon Hammer is a motivational speaker and the author of *The Positive Portions Food & Fitness Journal.* Having been overweight all her life, in 2003 Shannon adopted a holistic approach to health and weight loss that included keeping a daily food diary. As a result, she is maintaining an-over-100 pound weight loss. She wrote *The Positive Portions Food & Fitness Journal* after realizing a need in the market for a book that combines the proven effectiveness of a food diary with the daily encouragement of an inspirational book. She has been featured in many different segments of the media including national FOX TV. She currently lives in Redondo Beach, California, where she enjoys working out, writing fiction, and—now that's she willing to wear a bathing suit at a public level—going to the beach.

Full Circle

◆

Larry Koenig, Ph.D.—Bestselling Author, Educator, and Child-Behavior Expert

"The greatest discovery of my generation
is that a man can alter his life simply
by altering his attitude of mind."

—William James

I grew up in Boscobel, Wisconsin, a beautiful little river town of 2,500 people. It was the late 1950s, and life was really great there because as kids we could roam all over town; there was always some new adventure to discover. I had lots of friends, and in the winter, we'd go sledding or ice skating. In the summer we'd ride our bikes, go fishing, and swim. At just six years old I would walk to the community swimming pool by myself. In those days it was no big deal for kids to gallivant around because people watched out for one another's children.

Beginning in the first grade I would walk home from school almost every day and have lunch with my mother. In the springtime we'd have picnics in the yard or we'd eat out on the porch. There was always an abundance of squirrels and birds that joined us. In retrospect, my life in Boscobel, Wisconsin, was pretty good—a loving family in a quaint little town isolated from the turmoil in the world. It was almost perfect . . . almost.

You see, I was a sickly child, seriously ill with stomach problems. My stomach hurt much of the time, especially when I was at school, so though I loved to learn, I began to hate school. I also hated the way some of the teachers treated me. They were sure I was faking and often made me feel shame. Early on, I had wonderful teachers who instilled in me the belief that I was smart, which increased my desire to learn. But that all changed in the fifth grade. We were doing a square-dancing class, and I was just having the most fun when my teacher came up from behind me, grabbed my shoulders, and started violently shaking me. "Larry," she shouted. "We're not here to have fun! Do you understand? We are not here to have fun!" I'm sure I was being a typical boy and did something that annoyed her, but I'm also quite sure it didn't warrant her shaking me like she did and shaming me in front of my peers. The message I got was "school is not a place to enjoy, and I'm a bad person." It was also during this time that my stomachaches got progressively worse. My parents took me to the doctor several times, but they could never find anything wrong. "Oh, there's nothing wrong with him," the doctor told them. "He just doesn't like school."

Like I said, I was a typical boy who liked to do everything but homework. One Friday, my sixth-grade teacher growled in my ear, "If you don't have your homework by Monday you're going to get it." Well, I went home and forgot about it. I played with my friends all weekend, and when Monday morning rolled around I realized that I hadn't done my homework. My dad, who was a former principal, stuck his head through the doorway to my room and said, "Larry, get up. It's time to get ready for school."

"No, I have a stomachache," I complained. That was my trump card, but it didn't faze my dad.

Ironically, the more scared I got about not having my homework, my stomach began to *really* hurt. "I'm not going!" I protested. Dad tried to make me walk to school, but I wouldn't walk.

"Get in the car," he ordered, "I'm taking you." Dad nearly physically put me in the car. As we drove along getting closer and closer to the school, I started to bawl, frantically complaining that my stomach was hurting.

"Oh, all right!" my dad said while turning the car around. When we got home he told my mother to take me back to the doctor one more time, and if nothing was wrong then take me to a psychiatrist.

Fortunately, it was 1962 and a brand-new type of x-ray machine had recently been developed that had not been available earlier. They took x-rays, and unlike today, it took some time to get the results back. We were told to go home, that they would call us with the outcome. When they finally called, my mom answered the phone. "Mrs. Koenig," they said. "You've got to come now. It's urgent." So the whole family went straight to the clinic. My dad, my two brothers, and I waited in the car while my mom went in. When she came out, she was holding two giant manila x-ray envelopes and tears were streaming down her face. "We've have to go to the hospital in Madison," she said. "Something's wrong."

Basically, I had been living with a duodenum that was twice as big as my stomach, and I needed surgery. The duodenum is the first section of the small intestine and is normally about one-quarter the size of the stomach. No wonder I had stomachaches, and they tended to get worse when under stress. That's why they intensified at school.

When I was in St. Mary's Hospital in Madison, there was a young surgeon talking to my parents. They had stepped out in the hallway so I couldn't hear, but I heard everything, especially when the doctor told them that I only had a 50/50 chance of surviving the surgery. My parents were noticeably distraught, yet I was overcome by a strange peace. "Look," I told them, "it doesn't matter whether I live or die, because God is going to take care of me." Then, during surgery, while under anesthesia, Jesus came to me and said, "I've saved you. Come follow me."

Now, what you must understand is that I had never heard those words before in my life. I had no comprehension of "salvation" or "saved." I had never, ever heard those words. And the message that permeated me was more than just, "I have saved your life physically." It was, "I've saved your soul. Come follow me." It was something that I knew instinctively. How, at eleven years old, did I know that when I'd never heard the concept before? I don't know. I just did.

Over the years I never forgot what happened to me in that hospital and really thought I was supposed to be a minister. I went to college and got a bachelor's degree in religion, but during that time, I took a part-time position at a local church and failed miserably at it. As a result, though I still wanted to serve God and help people, I concluded that working in the church as a minister wasn't what I was supposed to do. Finally, after much soul-searching I wound up with a postgraduate degree in counseling and began working as a therapist at a mental health center, in Panama City, Florida. I was also married with two children. With God on my side, a desire to help people, and the tools I learned in counseling, what could go wrong, right?

The long story cut short is my five-year marriage crashed and burned. There were no affairs or things like that. My ex-wife simply decided she didn't want to be married to me any longer. We both had some serious issues and were a long way from our home in Wisconsin. Within six months I was married again to a nurse doing a mental health internship where I was counseling. When you get divorced and you have two small kids, you're all alone and in a lot of pain. Then, when someone comes along and falls in love with you, that feels awfully, awfully good. Now, you are validated and have someone to be with.

We were married for ten years with one child when I found out that she was having an affair with a doctor. One thing I told myself was that I would never lose a second family. When you go through the emotional pain of losing a family, you never, ever want to go through that kind of pain again. Come hell or high water, I was keeping this marriage together. I tried everything I knew to save the marriage, but in the end, she said, "I want a divorce," and married the doctor. Of course, she got custody of my daughter. I was all alone again. Then, as if everything I just told you wasn't enough, I abruptly lost my job without warning, leaving me broke. The judge had assessed $1,000 a month for child support and my bills before that were $1,800 a month. That's $2,800 not counting gas or food.

I felt totally and completely destitute. Not only was I financially broke, but I was emotionally broke as well, feeling like a complete loser. I had lost two families. I was thirty-five years old and had nothing. I had an old beat-up car that I was lucky to gas up just enough to get me across town and back. But the worst of it wasn't the financial thing. The worst of it was the emotional bankruptcy, where I saw myself as a total failure. Every time I looked in the mirror I saw a loser looking back. It was no good at that point to try and blame anyone else because what good was that going to do? Jesus appearing to me in the hospital seemed so long ago. Where was God now? Sure, He saved my life and my soul, but could He resurrect this mess that was my life?

I remember one night sitting alone in the house. It was nearly empty and had that vacant feel. It was a perfect reflection of my life. I was sitting there and said to myself, "You created this mess, Larry. If you are going to live through this and make it out, then you can't allow negative emotions to destroy you. You are going to have to do whatever it takes to become 100 percent positive. You're going to have to get around some other positive people. Go to a church. Read books. Listen to tapes. You are going to have to do whatever it takes to turn this around; otherwise, you're gonna die. You're not going to live through this. There's no way you are going to live through this." I knew this as certain as I knew the sun was going to come up in the morning.

And that is exactly what I did. I got involved with a church and forced myself to be positive. I listened to motivational tapes from different speakers and read good books of other people's victory over struggles. There's real power in listening to tapes and reading books, because when you have nothing for yourself, you must rely on other sources. You absolutely have to. When you are feeling good in life and everything is going well and you're filled up, you really don't seemingly need much outside of yourself. But when life knocks you back, you have to rely on the wisdom and enthusiasm of other people.

I told myself, "Larry, if you have to, fake it until you make it." I had to fake it because I couldn't say, "Oh, look at my wonderful life. Look at how well I've done or what a great person I am, or look at my accomplishments," because there were none. I couldn't look at material things because I didn't have those. As far as self-esteem went, there was none of that to rely on either. All the evidence said that I didn't have what it takes, yet I refused to give up on myself or on relationships. As I began to surround myself with the positive and force myself to put one foot in front of the other and keep going, even faking it sometimes, my situation began to change.

I found work. Then, after allowing myself sufficient time to heal, I met Nydia, my soul mate, best friend, and wife of twenty-three years. She has, hands down, been the person who's had the most powerful effect on my life. But in order for me to connect with her I had to get repaired to a certain point. I wasn't completely whole, because none of us are, but I was whole enough to be able to give of myself and not be needy.

Nydia is a very kind, healing type of person, and it was healing just to be around her. To touch her was healing. We fell deeply in love and got married. She had two kids. I had my three, so there were five kids between us. When we got married, all we had were debt and bills and not enough income. We'd be sitting at the table and the phone would ring. Bill collectors. We didn't have a lot of money to do things so we did the only thing we could do. We took walks, lots and lots of walks. Every evening we'd walk. We'd just walk and we'd talk for miles at a time. We'd share our dreams and really connected on a spiritual level.

It was during those times that it came to me what I was supposed to do with my life. I wanted to encourage kids, parents, and teachers, and I had ideas. It started with the vision of creating the Up with Youth rallies. These would be rallies for kids on Saturdays sponsored by local hospitals and TV channels. The rallies would consist of activities that encouraged kids in their struggles, gave them self-esteem, showed them how to stay away from drugs and alcohol, and helped them connect with other positive kids. Well, the program was so successful that as many as 500 kids would show up per rally, and we held them all over the United States for a number of years.

The Up with Youth rallies evolved into encouraging parents and teachers through my Smart Discipline seminars. I never want any child to go through what I did back in Boscobel, Wisconsin. Over the past twenty years I've taught tens of thousands of teachers globally how to get kids to want to learn from and cooperate with them. Everything that I teach is what I would have wanted from the teachers who treated me badly, and what I did get from some of the teachers who taught me well.

I must point out that when we got married, Nydia had a good job in the medical field and was completely supportive of me when I took the risk of stepping out and doing my own thing. I could never do what I do without her love and support through the lean years as well as the good years.

The difference in my struggles now and then is now I have the experience of knowing that whatever comes my way, with God's help, I can make it through. Do I still get stressed out at times? Absolutely. But it's stress with the knowledge that I will get through. I still have a vision for the future. We must always be stretching and growing. I'm still looking for bigger and more effective ways of helping children grow up and be successful in life. Some things you can't fix, but you can *always* create something new.

I can remember just a couple years ago a TV personality called me for an interview. When I got to the interview she said to me,

"I was talking to one of my friends and she asked who I was interviewing today. I told her it was you and she said, 'Why are you interviewing that loser?'" This was someone who knew me back when I was totally down and out. To go from where I was to where I am today is a total do-over miracle. It really is.

Larry Koenig, Ph.D., is the creator of Smart Discipline— America's most widely used system of discipline. His work has been featured on PBS, NPR, and in *People* magazine, *Parents* magazine, *Woman's World* magazine, and the Associated Press. His book, *Smart Discipline* (HarperCollins, 2004) is in seven languages and *Smart Discipline for the Classroom* (Corwin, 2007) is now in its fourth edition. His latest release, *Smart Discipline for Teachers of Young Children* is assisting teachers all over the world. To learn more about Larry's books and seminars, check out www.SmartDiscipline.org.

A Little Contour, a Lot of Courage

◆

Laura Geller—Makeup Artist

"Big shots are only little shots
who keep shooting."

—Christopher Morley

I was born in the Bronx in 1958 and lived there until I was seven when my mom said, "We got to get out of here. We got to make a better life for our kids." So, our family moved to Springvale, a small town within Rockland County, New York. My dad was a salesman of men's overcoats and suits. Geller, the Happy Fella, everyone called him. And he was a great salesman. His love of sales and love of people really molded me into who I am today.

All through school I was interested in beauty. In fact, I was infatuated with it. It wasn't makeup per se that I was interested in, but what makeup could do. The women on my block who I looked up to were always very fashion forward. They were women who made themselves up and painted their faces. My mom, on the other hand, was not one of these women. I suppose you might call her a "plain Jane." She would wear red lipstick and a little pancake on her face, and that was about it. It's funny because all the girls whose moms wore makeup weren't interested in the stuff. But I would think, "I can't believe this. What's wrong with you? Don't you want to go through your mother's makeup?" So these women took me under their wings since they knew I was interested, and they always painted my face, whether it was for my sweet sixteen or my prom.

When high school was over I planned to do what most girls my age did, learn secretarial skills. One day Jane, a friend of mine, said quite bluntly, "What are you doing?"

"I'm actually going upstate, and I'm going to go to secretarial school," I said.

"Why would you do that? You love makeup." Then she added, "I'm going to beauty school for hair design."

"There's no way you're going to beauty school," I said.

"I am, and you need to come with me, because I think you'll do really well!" And, so it was. I went. I am so thankful to her now. It was like she gave me a license to go and do what I really wanted.

Once I got to beauty school, though, I learned that they didn't offer a makeup program; it was mainly hair design. But, in those days, in order to get your cosmetology license, you had to go through the program. After talking to the owner of the school, he became really interested in learning how to further educate me, so he found out where there were makeup courses. That's how I wound up taking classes at the School of Visual Arts in Manhattan.

Once again, though, I didn't get what I signed up for. I wound up in a theatrical makeup course, learning how to put bald caps on and creating wounds. So, not exactly pink eye shadow and sparkly lipstick. I almost dropped the class, but fortunately for me, I stuck it out. The class wound up being one of the best classes I could've taken. Instead of just teaching me how to apply makeup, I learned how to do things with makeup. I learned about bone structure, and how you take someone from twenty to eighty years old. I learned how to transform people.

This was how I got started. After lots of study, famed makeup artist Herman Buchman took me under his wing and made me his assistant. I traveled with him doing makeup on films. Then I began working on a television interview show doing makeup for celebrities. It was incredible. I had the opportunity to do makeup for legends such as Ginger Rogers, Audrey Hepburn, Henry Fonda, Robert Mitchum, Jane Russell, and Jessica Tandy. It was like a dream come true.

While doing these makeup gigs I realized I needed a steady job, too. So I got a job at a place that sold theater and film makeup where celebrities came to buy their own stuff. All these luminaries would come in, and I would help explain the products to them. It was amazing. The store also had a brand of street makeup, or regular makeup, and all of a sudden I started realizing that this is what I originally wanted—to put on pink eye shadow and sparkly lipstick. I started doing makeup there privately in special makeup rooms. I charged people twenty-five dollars and taught them how to do their face. It was great because I was combining my knowledge of theater and film makeup, but I was transforming the average woman.

All of a sudden I found myself doing makeup sales, and everything I learned from my dad came roaring back. I actually stayed at that makeup store because I was enjoying myself so much. Everything was going well. I had a steady job and was doing private makeup sessions, but then I got fired.

I'd wanted to take two weeks off to go to Spain. I'd always wanted to study the culture and beauty of Spain but never went earlier because I wanted stability and an income. So I finally worked up the courage to ask my boss for an additional week off. I said, "Look, I know I have a vacation coming and it's a week, but I'd like to take an additional week. You don't have to pay me." He was a little reluctant, but my boss went for it. The next day, however, when I arrived at work I found out I could take off as much time as I wanted. I was fired.

I nearly fell over. I had never been fired before. I didn't know what to do. I had worked there for ten years. Of course, I went sobbing to one of my friends, completely brokenhearted. But at the same time I was inspired to do something big. I didn't go to Spain after all. Instead, I went full speed ahead into starting my own business. I rented an apartment and set up a little studio. I learned the hard way, though, that there is a big difference between City Center, where the makeup shop was, and 55th Street and 8th Avenue, where my new place was. My clients were afraid to come to my neighborhood, Hell's Kitchen, which wasn't as safe and popular then as it is now. After a couple of years of this, I realized I had to do something. I mean, I didn't have the skill set or business education behind me to know how to open a business.

At the time, I was dating a man who really helped me. He set me up with a friend of his who had a salon on Madison Avenue, and I rented out her basement. I borrowed some money from friends and family and opened up shop, Laura Geller Makeup. Almost immediately I was flooded. I didn't have my own store, but my name was on the window at the salon, which was official enough for me.

Business was booming, and I started selling makeup products in addition to doing makeup because my clients wanted to know where to buy it. So I bought some manufactured products and labeled them. It was the first step to manufacturing my own products. Everything was great and I was really happy, finally doing what I felt I was made to do. I had been investing all this money into renovating the basement. Then life, again, did the unexpected. The salon owner saw that I was making a lot of money and was busy, and she decided not to renew my contract after the first year. I lost all the money invested in the renovations and had to find a new place.

I had built up a base of East Side clientele, but I moved to the West Side and set up in a clothing boutique. Eventually, though, I realized that my clients wanted me to have my own store and wanted privacy. In 1993 I opened my own shop.

I have to tell you, though, all those years of not knowing where I was going to end up and making mistakes led me to where I am today. That's part of my story, that I learned by default. I love that I didn't go right from one place to the next because someone made it easy for me. It's part of my appreciation for where I am today.

In order to open the new store I had to borrow money from everyone. I didn't know how to get a loan in those days. It was humbling to ask family and friends for money, but I did what I had to do. After I got everything together, I landed this great place on Lexington Avenue, and I still have that store today. Since I didn't have the business background, I hired an accountant to handle my books. Everything seemed good. I paid my two employees on time, every time. Things were working.

After a couple of years, I started getting letters saying that I hadn't paid my taxes. I asked my accountant, and he said he would take care of it, no problem. I really didn't know how to smell a rat, but I talked to my dad about it. He thought to himself, *Something's very wrong here and I'm going to send my friend in, who is an efficiency expert. He'll get a lay of the land.* Come to find out, my taxes weren't paid. I had made the mistake of giving my accountant blank checks to pay taxes, and he wasn't using them for that. When it was all said and done, I owed between $80,000 and $100,000. I was so frustrated and scared. It felt like I always kept running into these big bumps in the road along the way. Things would be going well, and then boom! Another kink! Would life ever go smoothly for me?

Something I really learned, though, was that you have to keep an eye on your books. Never just take someone's word for it. Luckily, a friend set me up with a real accounting firm that helped me negotiate all the debt. Those years were a struggle; sometimes I only had enough money to pay my two employees and the bills, and I couldn't enjoy the fruits of my labor. Friends and family came through again and loaned me money so I could keep afloat. Eventually, I got caught up and back on track.

One day, my PR person put me in touch with the health and beauty woman for QVC. She came into the store and asked me what I would do if I came on QVC. I said, "I'm known for contour. I've created a contour kit because women need to know how to sculpt their face. That's what I do best. I know anatomy."

"Put it together and I'll come back," she said.

So I did. She came back and asked how much I'd charge. I said ten dollars, and she ordered 750 of them. I was so excited and freaked out at the same time. I called up my mother and asked if she still had an extra table in the garage. We got a bunch of friends together and packed up the kits. I didn't even know fulfillment houses existed. I did it all myself with the help of friends. It took two weeks. I had a friend in Florida print out inserts, and we wrapped them in purple tissue and stuffed them in bags supplied by a friend's husband.

So I sent the bags to QVC and they had me come on the air to sell them. I was so nervous I thought I was going to have an anxiety attack. But I went out there and did a demonstration. I sold out in five minutes. I got offstage and basically fell on the floor. I had never sold 750 of anything in my whole life. I cried like a baby.

A week after going back to work the fax machine started making noise, and I had an order for 1,250 more units. I called my mom again and told her to get everyone together a second time. We packed up the kits, and I sold out again. I just kept selling out—I seemed to be a natural.

But everything wasn't quite that simple. The PR people wanted 50 percent of everything I made on QVC because they thought they were the agents that had brought me success. So I talked to some lawyers and we negotiated it down to 10 percent. I really didn't think I would be at QVC forever, so I didn't think signing 10 percent would be that bad. I had to do something in order to stay on QVC. So I did.

Years later, I was still signing monthly checks to the PR people who hadn't really done anything. I couldn't decide what frustrated me more, what the bookkeeper did to me years earlier or what these people were doing to me now. Or that I'd allowed it to happen because I was too naive. Well, I called up the PR woman who had intimidated me before and told her I wanted out of the contract because it wasn't fair. There was a lawsuit. I spent a lot of money and had to pay them off, but it was worth it to have them out of my hair. I had been so scared to talk to them that it went on too long. I just had to learn the hard way. I didn't know that I could have talked to QVC early on to see if they would put me on air without the help of the PR people. I guess I was just scared to try on my own.

Still, all the ups and downs I've had over the years, getting to where I am now—it was all worth it. I get letters from women who watch me and think, *You know, she's not size four and she looks pretty. I stopped doing my face because I thought I wasn't worthy of looking good. Now I'm doing it because she made it so simple and I can understand her message. This has changed my life.* I can't begin to tell you what that does to me to this day. I never get tired of it. I learned a lot of things the hard way, but I never gave up trying. Instead of letting these catastrophic events crush me, like being fired or having a bookkeeper steal from me, I used them as opportunities to try anew. Eventually, I got it right, and I'm on cloud nine.

Before launching her own company, Laura Geller was the makeup artist for some of the theater industry's rising stars. Her work also graced the small screen, including on-air talent at CBS, NBC, AMC, and HBO. Today, Laura is most often seen in front of the camera through her many QVC appearances in the United States, the UK, and Germany. Her exceptional ability to connect with her viewers has been a key to her success and led to a cult following for her brand. When it comes to today's beauty, Laura Geller has an uncanny knack for knowing what works and what wows. She's masterminded an ingenious collection of multitasking color cosmetics that give every woman a fresh and fabulous look, which she pairs with informative, no-nonsense how-to advice. To find out more about her company and makeup line, visit www.laurageller.com.

Three Feet from the Ditch

◆

John Manda—Weight-Loss and Nutritional Life-Reinvention

"The great thing in this world is not so much where
we are, but in what direction we are moving."

—Oliver Wendell Holmes

I was just fifty-two years old, but even the simple, everyday, mundane tasks had become impossible for me. My wonderful wife, Mandy, out of the kindness of her heart, and knowing what I was going through, had taken over most of the chores. I could not even take the garbage to the street because I couldn't make it back up the slight incline on our driveway. You see, though I'm only five feet six inches tall, I weighed nearly 400 pounds. When we'd go places that required us to walk, Mandy often drove and dropped me off at the door of the establishment because it was so difficult for me to walk from the parking lot. My quality of life was terrible, not only for me but also for my wife. We had friends that couldn't bring themselves to come around me any longer. They later told me it was breaking their hearts to see me dying in front of them, so they just kind of stayed away. I became a shut-in. In early 2008 when I was still able to work, right before things really began to spiral downhill, I had to wake up an hour or so early every morning to sit on a heating pad just to relax my back enough so I could get up, take a bath, and hobble to work. Eventually, I couldn't even do that. Toward the end, before I started my do over, not a day went by that I didn't at least stop once and picture what it would feel like to die.

I thought about death all the time. Where would I be when it happened? How would it happen? Would it be a heart attack or a stroke? They were terrible imaginings perpetuated by fear. I used to worry about whether or not I'd be close to Mandy. Would we be away from each other? Would I get to see her before I breathed my last breath? When I disclosed to Mandy the feelings I was having about my impending death, she told me that she'd long ago realized that she was going to be a widow very early in her life, that she was preparing herself emotionally to be alone. That broke my heart.

At this point, my self-esteem and self-image was at its lowest. I basically had none. Though on the surface I appeared happy and jolly, deep inside, I hated myself every time I looked in the mirror. Part of it was because of my own failures and part of it was because of the way people treated me. There are many people out there who treat morbidly obese people differently. They view them as less than or lower than. They assume that you're out of control and living life in a derelict manner. They see in you all the negative things they don't want to be. I've been looked at with disdain and disgust and felt it every time. Once I was on an airplane and had an aisle seat. As I walked toward my seat to sit down, there was a lady sitting in the middle seat. When she saw me coming, she gave me the nastiest look and then scooted herself off to one side in an extreme manner and sat that way the whole time. The way she'd positioned herself that day, the message I got was she didn't want to touch me. It was almost like if she touched me, some of my fat might rub off on her. She wouldn't speak. It was terrible. She was totally disgusted with me. It's a look you can't mistake. I tried to ignore it for a long time, but I just couldn't. It's impossible, and it has a demoralizing effect.

Things got progressively worse until Christmas 2008, and Mandy and I both knew I couldn't go on like this. It was no longer just that I was a "fat" man. Now, I couldn't function in society, and my life was in danger. A decision had to be made, but for me, really it was more than just making a decision to lose weight. A person that gets to my stage is someone who's had a whole life of profoundly dysfunctional habits that have become deeply rooted in their personality.

God had been dealing with me about my life and lifestyle—I realized that losing weight for me would be much more that just shedding the pounds. It would be about getting to those root causes. That meant honestly addressing who I *really* was, who I'd become, and why I'd let myself become what I was. I knew the life I was living was not God's best for me, nor was it who I wanted to be. Usually, for sustained weight loss to happen, a person must develop a healthy lifestyle both emotionally and physically. The two overlap. You can't really have one without the other. It also takes support—a lot of support.

When I had reached the critical stage, and it was either take action or die, Mandy said she wanted to take the journey with me. Mandy's always been very supportive and has handled my weight issues carefully, gently, and compassionately. But it's been hard on her. Over the course of our marriage, I feel like my weight issues enabled her to become overweight herself. She had little motivation to take care of her body because her husband wasn't doing anything about his. So, she gained weight with me.

When we made the choice to take this journey together, we knew we would need additional support, so we joined Weight Watchers. There was something magical about our group. It was a good group of both men and women. Traditionally, Weight Watchers doesn't have a lot of men, but we had seven or eight men in our group. And these men and women were very positive-minded. They would encourage, motivate, educate, and push us not to give up. Now, Mandy's lost fifty pounds and looks incredible. She wants to lose fifty more. I've lost 100 pounds and feel great, but I still have 100 to go.

When I began my do over, I was in such bad shape that I couldn't work out or do any kind of exercise. From January to August 2009 I couldn't really exercise. But by August I had lost enough weight to start exercising. From August to January 2010 is when I really focused on the workouts combined with the lifestyle change—learning how to eat properly and learning what made me eat. Why did I overeat? What was the motivation? I learned a lot about myself. I learned that I ate out of boredom. I identified that watching television, although it was something that I enjoyed, was a time of great boredom that produced a desire to eat.

The first thing, like I said, was self-examination, being brutally honest with myself. We have to be willing to confess to ourselves who we really are, to stop all of the deception. I had to rebuild my life from the bottom up, starting with the foundation of truth about myself. I've been under construction and remodeling since January 2009. I had to identify my weaknesses and then be willing to deal with them and make qualitative changes. Again, it's much more than just losing weight! Why do most people fail at sustaining their weight loss? In my opinion, it's because they go on the wrong kinds of plans. Diets are always failures waiting to happen. In most cases all we are doing is denying ourselves caloric intake for a while. Of course, the body will naturally drop some weight. And then, after that, we've lost weight but we haven't learned anything about who we really are. I've had to learn how to overcome my weaknesses by getting to the root causes for why I was the way I was.

Going all the way back to my early childhood, I can't remember not having a weight problem. When I think back, I see emotional issues. I hate to sound cliché, but my father never really accepted me for who I was. He always wanted me to be someone that I wasn't. We didn't share a lot in common. He was an avid sportsman and I was an avid book reader. He liked the outside. I liked to stay inside. My father never felt he could relate to me, so he basically dropped me. My mother tried to encourage me, but she was battling her own emotional demons. She was plagued with depression from being in a very unhappy and unhealthy marriage. It was loveless. I can remember as a Cub Scout in elementary school, I was the only scout in the pack whose mother brought him to the meetings. My father wouldn't have anything to do with me. He wouldn't invest any time in me.

From early on, I learned to use food as a narcotic to sedate me and make me happy. I loved food. We were in the food business, so we were surrounded by it. We owned Manda Fine Meats, a $36 million-a-year corporation that produced sausage, ham, roast beef, and a variety of deli items. My grandfather founded it, and my father was the president and CEO until he passed away several years ago. We had an abundance of food. So much so, that in elementary school it was not uncommon when we came back from the holidays for my teachers to ask me to stand up and tell the class what we had for Thanksgiving or Christmas dinner. It was so much food that the average child was never really exposed to it. My classmates would sit there drooling. This also reinforced to me some acceptance, which made me further indulge myself with food.

In addition, I grew up an only child and didn't have kids in my neighborhood to play with. I had to occupy myself, and food was always easy for me to get hold of and satisfied me. Between being surrounded by food and using it as the narcotic of choice, weight gain was inevitable. Neither my father nor my mother was overweight, though it did run in our family, but nothing like mine. Mine went from overweight to obesity to morbid obesity.

But thank God, today I am no longer that person. Though our journey has really just begun, and it's not an easy road, both Mandy's and my transformation has been nothing less than startling. People walk up to us on a regular basis amazed. They can't believe it's us.

Before, I was a sad, lethargic, self-loathing invalid, fixated on death. Now I have excitement, hope, and unlimited energy! For the first time in my life when I look in the mirror, I actually like the person looking back. I have a level of confidence now that I just didn't have before. And remember those friends who couldn't bear to be around me? Now, instead of repelling people, people are actually drawn to me because they can sense hope. One couple told me, "Since you've lost the weight, you have become such an inspiration to us that we want to be around you more than ever before. We feel like every time we're with you we leave with something that helps us." I'm like, "Good! Good!" When people sense you are confident and that you feel good about yourself, that you know where you are going, you exude that type of attitude.

And the physical energy I have! It's amazing! Strength, endurance, all of it is there. When I walk on the treadmill for more than an hour, I never forget that not that long ago I couldn't do five minutes. The other day at work, a coworker and I had to walk somewhere. She is a young woman who's probably twenty-five years younger than me. She said, "John, you're killing me."

"What's wrong?" I asked.

"I can't walk this fast."

I was thinking, *Praise God!* I told her that in December 2008 I couldn't walk at all!

"You're unbelievable!" she said.

That's the way it is now. But before I wrap up, I'd like to leave you with a few important things that have really helped me.

First, protect yourself from negative people. Because food was a mechanism to fight depression, disillusionment, and unhappiness, if I encountered a difficult person—someone who was critical or mean-spirited—just one unkind or harsh word could trigger me into an overeating binge. Part of my journey has been to identify certain people in my life that were not good for me, that were poisonous. I made the decision that I'd pull away from them and not let them be a part of my life. And I've successfully done that. I view negativity as a form of cancer.

Likewise, positive, encouraging people are a source of fuel. Surround yourself with them. This is one reason why our Weight Watchers group has been so vital to our long-term success. Just an encouraging word from someone can go a long way. Once, my ophthalmologist inspired me tremendously, although it was just a brief encounter. He hadn't seen me in a while and was amazed at how different I looked and wanted to know what I was doing. I told him about the journey Mandy and I were on.

On the way out, he turned to me, looked me in the eyes and said, "I'm very proud of you, John, but I want to say one thing; remain diligent. Diligence is the vehicle that will help you attain the success you are seeking." I haven't forgotten that. Those few words made a huge difference.

The second piece of advice is to stay humble. Remember: you can't reach your goals alone and you can always fall backward. It's a journey for life. I have some dear friends whose son went through a time in his life when he got into drugs and alcohol. He became very involved in AA (Alcoholics Anonymous), and I remember one day he said, "John, no matter how far you go, no matter how great your success, you are always only three feet from the ditch and can always fall back into it. It never goes away. You have to keep yourself out of the ditch." I've never forgotten those words either.

Finally, I guess the best thing about my weight-loss journey was hearing Mandy recently say, "I've watched your weight and lifestyle change, and I've stopped worrying about you dying. I know the changes you've made are for real."

A gifted speaker and writer, John Manda is an inspiration to everyone he meets.

A Patented Do Over

◆

Lori Greiner—Inventor, Entrepreneur, and Playwright

"The greatest risk is the risk of riskless living."

—Stephen Covey

I grew up in downtown Chicago and never thought I'd be doing what I'm doing. I mean, who puts "inventor" down on their life's mission statement? I wanted to be a filmmaker. That was the one thing that I thought I'd be. My mind is very creative and visual. Whenever I'd hear music, for example, I didn't just hear the melody, I'd see a movie taking place in my mind—the scenes, the characters. I have the ability to create ideas and visualize the finished product in my head. I see things. Because of my creativity, the writer spirit was always alive in me. I would write things either on paper or in my mind, and the films would just be playing over in my head. I loved plays and the theater, too. I loved anything that involved telling a story.

I majored in communications and got a degree in journalism, television, and film. For a while, I worked for the *Chicago Tribune* and learned that journalism was probably not right for me. What I really wanted was to work in film. So, I went to work freelancing in film and video production, and I really enjoyed that too, but it was more challenging to be in Chicago. I'd work intensely for a few days on a film or video and then not work for a week or two. It was very erratic and inconsistent.

Because of this inconsistency, I began selling jewelry on the side to supplement my income. My mother suggested it, actually. There was a show in Chicago for a particular line of jewelry, and she said, "Let's go to it." While at the show she said, "Why don't you ask them if you can sell it?" I said "Okay." So, it just happened. It was happenstance. Once I got into it, I'd go to New York to the different jewelry shows to purchase product, then return to Chicago and sell it. I did this between stints in film and video.

During this time I also wrote my first play, and it won a prestigious award for playwriting excellence. I was so excited; it was what I'd dreamed of, and it was so wonderful to see something that I'd created in my mind actually come to life on the stage. I started working at a theater in Chicago reading scripts for them, writing my own plays, and learning more about the art and craft of playwriting. Doing the creative thing was driving me, bringing me fulfillment, but selling jewelry on the side was making my real income. Then, I hired a salesperson to sell the jewelry for me.

If you can believe it, I had also started to write a book that I called *Fairytales for the Nineties*. (I have always been a huge multitasker.) It was a modern-day fairytale, because when I looked at fairytales from way back I thought they were rather chauvinistic and kind of frightening. I just felt they needed to be updated. One day, I was standing in line at Barnes & Noble and I saw this book at the checkout counter. I noticed it was a *New York Times* bestseller and that it was called *Politically Correct Bedtime Stories*. I thought, *Oh, my God, that's my book! I should've done it faster and gotten it out there.*

Shortly thereafter I came up with the idea for my first product invention—my earring organizer. Because I sold jewelry, I used to make my own fixtures that I'd display the jewelry on. I'd already created a very simple organizer, but I took it to a much higher level. I was talking with a friend about earrings and how hard they are to store. Earrings are usually in boxes and all jumbled up. It's hard to find the mate, or the backs come off. *Wouldn't it be great,* I thought, *if women had a single place to hang all their earrings?* Then almost instantly, I saw the whole product in my mind, just like I saw movies or plays. It just came to me very quickly in that conversation what it would be like. I could see the entire product: It would have sliding earring stands with one right behind the other so you could see all your earrings hanging at a quick glance. Just slide one out to the right or left. It all just came to me.

I remembered my book experience, how I'd waited and it was too late. So when I thought of the idea for my earring organizer, which was my very first product, I said, "I'm just going to jump on it."

The motivational part of my story is about turning dreams into reality—having an idea, a movie, or product, and then taking action to make it come to life. I set about figuring out how to do it, and I did it by myself. I figured out all the steps necessary to make this product happen. I took out an enormous loan, went to a patent attorney, and applied for a patent.

Before I took out the loan, I did my homework. I found out how much money it would take to make my product, and I did market research. Yes, it was a risk, but not a stupid risk. There's a difference. Part of the research consisted of going around to different neighborhoods in Chicago with a prototype model. I took it to all different kinds of neighborhoods and literally stopped ladies walking down the street to ask if they'd look at my product. I asked questions like, "Do you like this? What would you pay for it? Would you buy it?" Most were really wonderful. Sure, some just walked by, but many came over. They told me their thoughts. I compiled all that information. That's what convinced me the product would be successful.

After I took out the loan, I set about making my earring organizer. It's an injection-molded product, so it requires tooling and a special manufacturing plant, which I found. Then I went about selling it. That was the most difficult part. I called stores all across the country again, and again, and again. Then I took my organizers and personally went to twenty-one cities in twenty-eight days to talk to store buyers.

Eventually, I got JC Penney to buy, along with some other outlets. JC Penney was the biggest and instrumental in my success. After a lot of hard work, my organizers tested well during the holiday season, and I got some large purchase orders. I called it the For Your Ears Only earring organizer.

When I first tried to get on QVC they sent my organizers back. Undeterred, I went to QVC UK, and I got on. They sold great! In fact, I sold out! Then they connected me to QVC USA. I'm probably the only person on Earth to do it that way and go backward, but who cares. It worked, and I sold out again! I was ecstatic and hugely relieved. QVC then wanted more ideas and more products. That was the beginning of me creating more products.

I'm a risk taker. It's my nature, and I'd taken an enormous risk. I think it's the nature of all inventors to think that everybody will love their product, that everybody needs their product. But that's not necessarily so. I'd taken out that enormous loan, and if I hadn't been successful, I would have had a huge amount to pay off. So I was extremely excited and extremely relieved. Since then it has been a very exciting journey. Today, I've created more than 250 products, have more than 100 patents, and have many more pending. I've learned so much along the way and have broken through so many obstacles and barriers. Best of all, I have had AMAZING adventures and experiences! So many stories to tell!

In thinking about what was my most difficult product to make, that would have to be my Silver Safekeeper Tri-mirror

Jewelry Cabinet. I'm extra proud of it because to create it was really a feat. It's very difficult engineering-wise. Many people told me it would be impossible to make, but we pulled it off. I would say that most of my inventions have been hits, although some of them haven't been. I do have a pretty high track record. When I'm trying to decide on a new product, I go with my gut as to what I think is right—what's needed, what's good, what's a better way, what people would like.

If somebody is thinking about following their dream or passion, I'd say be smart, but go for it. If you have a passion for something and you really apply yourself, you can make it happen. I hate the words "I can't." To me, there isn't any such thing. Instead, it should be, "How can I?" or "What do I need to do?" If someone possesses that attitude, they can make great things happen.

There are many different stories in this book of many different types of do overs. My story is about creating a new life by creating an idea and then taking a risk. I hear people sometimes say, "Oh, I'd love to do this or that," but then they come up with all these excuses for why they can't take action. I think to be successful, a person has to really want it more than anything else and then practically apply themselves to whatever it is they want and start tearing down any obstacles as to why it won't work or they can't do it. They have to be willing to be a hard worker and willing to put in an enormous amount of time and energy. A lot of people have great ideas but they want someone else to do the work for them. I understand that people have busy lives. I get it. But if you want to follow your dream and make it a reality, at some point you take control, break out of your comfort zone, and take action.

In addition to being the creative force behind her company, For Your Ease Only, Inc., Lori has also accumulated quite a following as a TV personality. She has her very own show, *Clever & Unique Creations by Lori Greiner,* which airs live each month on QVC. Lori's products can also be found in several retail stores and catalogs and have been featured in magazines such as *O, The Oprah Magazine, InStyle, Family Circle, Woman's Day, Redbook, People, Self, Success,* and the *Financial Times.* To learn more about Lori Greiner and her products, go to www.Lorigreiner.com.

Again and Again . . . and Again

◆

Anne Sullivan and Helen Keller— Teacher, Student, and World Changers

> "Keep on beginning and failing.
> Each time you fail, start all over again,
> and you will grow stronger until you have accomplished
> a purpose—not the one you began with perhaps,
> but one you'll be glad to remember."
>
> —Anne Sullivan

Sometimes the obstacles in our lives are so daunting that it takes "doing over" again and again and again. In such cases, life reinvention is about seeing failure as a stepping-stone, never giving up, staying the course, and making whatever adjustments are necessary to reach the goal. Anne Sullivan and Helen Keller are two such people. Life reinvention and success eventually came for them, but it was only through sheer persistence and the willingness to push through incredible odds, skeptics, personal tragedy, and their own imperfections.

Helen Keller was born a normal, healthy child on June 27, 1880, on a small northwest Alabama cotton plantation. When she was nineteen months old, Helen fell ill with scarlet fever. For many days Helen was expected to die. When the fever finally broke, Helen's family was relieved that their daughter had survived. Helen's mother soon noticed, though, that her daughter failed to respond when the dinner bell rang or when she passed her hand in front of her daughter's eyes. Helen had survived her illness, but it had ruthlessly stolen her hearing and her sight. Helen Keller had become both deaf and blind.

The decade that followed proved extremely difficult for Helen and her family. Frustrated and confused, Helen became uncontrollable, smashing dishes and lamps and terrorizing the whole household with her temper tantrums. Relatives regarded her as a monster and insisted she be institutionalized. But the Kellers wouldn't hear of it. After much counsel and searching, they eventually employed a young woman named Anne Sullivan to work with Helen.

Anne herself had learned to thrive on the jagged edges of disability and loss. By the age of five she had lost the majority of her sight. By the time Anne was ten, her mother had died and her father deserted her. She and her brother, Jimmie, lived in an orphanage where he died in his teenage years, leaving her completely alone.

Although she was able to read print for short periods of time, Anne read braille as well. She attended the Perkins Institution for the Blind and planned to be a teacher, but due to her poor eyesight, finding work was nearly impossible. When she received the offer to serve as Helen's teacher, she accepted.

Anne immediately started teaching Helen to finger spell. Her first word was *doll* to signify a present she had bought to give to Helen. The next word she taught Helen was *cake*. Although Helen could repeat these finger movements, she could not understand what they meant. And while Anne was laboring to help her understand, she also struggled to keep Helen's behavior under control. Like a wild animal, Helen had become accustomed to climbing onto the dinner table and eating with her hands from the plates of everyone seated there.

To improve Helen's behavior, she and Anne moved into a small cottage near the main house. Anne's attempts to improve Helen's table manners, and make her brush her hair and button her shoes, led to increasingly violent temper tantrums, which Anne addressed by refusing to finger spell on Helen's hands.

Over the weeks, Helen's behavior dramatically improved, and a bond between the two grew. Then, on April 5, 1887, a "miracle" breakthrough occurred. Up until that point, Helen had not fully understood the meaning of the words Anne would finger spell, but on that day, when Anne led her to the water pump, everything changed.

As Anne pumped the water over Helen's hand, she spelled out the word *water* into Helen's free hand. Something clicked in Helen's brain, and Anne could immediately see that she understood. Helen enthusiastically asked Anne for the name of the pump to be spelled on her hand and then the name of the trellis. All the way back to the house, Helen excitedly learned the names of everything she touched and also asked for Anne's name. Anne spelled the name *teacher* on Helen's hand. Within the next few hours, Helen learned the spelling of thirty new words.

From that point on, Helen's progress was astonishing. Her ability to learn was far beyond anything anyone had ever seen among the deaf and blind. Before long Anne was teaching Helen to read—first with raised letters and later with braille—then to write with both standard and braille typewriters.

Helen Keller went on to become the first deaf and blind person to enroll at an institution of higher learning. She graduated on June 28, 1904, from Radcliffe College, becoming the first deaf and blind person to earn a bachelor of arts degree. Helen found fame as an author of many inspiring books, as a lecturer, and as a representative of the American Foundation for the Blind. Consider her words:

> Difficulties meet us at every turn. They are the accompaniment of life. . . . The surest way to meet them is to assume that we are immortal and that we have a Friend who "slumbers not, nor sleeps," and who watches over us and guides us—if we but trust Him.
>
> With this thought strongly entrenched in our inmost being, we can do almost anything we wish and need not limit the things we think. We may help ourselves to all the beauty of the universe that we can hold. For every hurt there is recompense of tender sympathy. Out of pain grow the violets of patience and sweetness. The

marvelous richness of human experience would lose something of rewarding joy if there were no limitations to overcome. The hilltop hour would not be half so wonderful if there were no dark valley to traverse.[5]

Remember, that was written from someone who was both deaf and blind! If she could accomplish what she did in the face of such incredible obstacles, then we really have no excuses.

Anne Sullivan also received numerous awards for her amazing work with Helen. In 1957 *The Miracle Worker* was first performed. A drama portraying Anne Sullivan's success in communicating with Helen as a child, it first appeared as a live play and was eventually made into a full-length motion picture.

> "People seldom see the halting
> and painful steps by which the most
> insignificant success is achieved."
>
> —Anne Sullivan

[5] Helen Keller, *My Religion* (1927), quoted in Dale Carnegie, *Dale Carnegie's Scrapbook* (New York: Simon & Schuster, 1959), 114.

I See Possibilities

◆

Anson Williams—Actor, Director, and Entrepreneur

"You have to stand outside the box to see
how the box can be re-designed."

—Charles Handy

Growing up Anson Williams Heimlich in a Jewish/Hispanic neighborhood in East Los Angeles was more like bomba music than the Beach Boys. We weren't quite poor but were lower middle class. If there was anything I wanted in life outside of the basics, I had to get a job and earn it. I consider that a positive thing though, because my deeply rooted work ethic is what helped lay the foundation for success in my life.

In high school, I wasn't popular, nor was I unpopular. I could get a ride with the popular kids in their great cars, but I never got a window seat. The middle of the backseat was the best I could get in high school. It's ironic that I wound up playing Potsie on *Happy Days*. If you're familiar with the show, then you know that Potsie was a very popular high school guy. Because I wasn't the character Potsie in real life growing up, I based him on my observations of two friends of mine who were popular.

I never went to acting school in my life, but I loved singing, dancing, and acting, and would go to talent nights around Los Angeles. Years ago they would have nights at different locations around the city where anybody could go in and play instruments, sing, do musical skits, comedy, or whatever. I'd literally go to three or four of those a week. I wasn't very good, but I had this desire. One day I heard about an open audition for an Equity play at the Hollywood Masonic Temple on Hollywood Boulevard. Equity (or Actors' Equity Association) is a membership group that allows actors in training to credit theatrical work in Equity theaters toward eventual membership in Equity. Getting your Equity card is a big deal if you're serious about acting. So I went to the audition, waited for hours, and finally got my turn. It was very intimidating. I was in this room with an old, crusty piano player where I had to sing and dance. When I finished, the producer said, "You sang okay. You can't dance worth a flip, but you've got something. Would you be willing to be an apprentice? We'll pay you fifty dollars a week. We'll figure out a way to get you to Wichita, Kansas, for a play out there. If you last the summer, we'll give you an Equity contract and you'll be a member."

My first words were, "You're going to pay me?" It was true. They paid me. They wouldn't buy airline tickets to Wichita, but they paid for the gas. A group of us drove twenty-nine straight hours, stopping at truck stops along the way to shower. The first twenty-five dollars of every fifty went to the hotel. The other twenty-five paid for food and whatever else I needed for the week, which wasn't much because they owned us twenty-four hours a day. I'd be in the show and then after the show would work building the sets. But I lasted the whole summer and headed back from Kansas as an official actor, ready to receive my Equity card. This meant I could now stand in the Equity line at auditions instead of the non-Equity line. I went back to selling shoes but auditioned every chance I got.

After I had stood in line with hundreds of people and auditioned for many parts, I eventually got a part in the theater play *Victory Canteen* with music by the Sherman Brothers, who did the film *Mary Poppins*. When I got the part, I had forty-eight hours to learn a brand-new show—every song, every piece of dialogue, every dance step. I learned it and did the show for an extended period. Even though I was working in theater, I knew if I was going to get anywhere in this business, I needed an agent, a real Hollywood agent. Everyone told me it was next to impossible to get one. I would respond by saying, "Oh really?" Don't ever tell me something is impossible.

Refusing to listen to the pessimists, I bolted down to one of the biggest acting agencies in the world, IFA (International Famous Agency), which eventually merged with CMA (Creative Management Associates) to become ICM (International Creative Management). I charged into the offices and asked to see an agent. The receptionist asked me if I had an appointment.

I said, "No, but when someone is free I'll be here." She told me to get out, but I refused. She threatened to call security, but I wouldn't leave and politely waited six hours. Finally, an agent came out and said, "Come here!"

I stood up and walked over to him. "Are you an agent?" I asked.

"Yes," he said, and I immediately started selling him. He laughed and told me to come into his office. It was tiny, but I thought it was the Taj Mahal.

"Listen," he said, still chuckling, "I don't know if you're good or bad, and I don't have time to see that show you're in. However, we don't have a lot of people over eighteen that can do high school parts. So I tell you what. There's an audition for a show called *Owen Marshall: Counselor at Law.* They're casting high school football players for a segment. You get the part and we'll sign you."

"Great!" I said, determined somehow to get it.

As I mentioned, up to that point I'd only done musical comedy and had never had an acting lesson in my life. I had to audition for a high school football player who dies from an overdose of drugs. So I went down to Universal Studios, took the audition with a lot of other wannabes, and was amazed when I ended up getting the part. *Owen Marshall: Counselor at Law* starred Lee Majors and was directed by Steven Spielberg. The agent was true to his word, and I signed with one of the biggest agencies in Hollywood. That's a 100 percent true story, and it's an example for anyone in any occupation—you've got to get out of the box in life. You've got to take control and take some risks.

After I signed with the agency, I got a concerned boyfriend part on a *Hallmark Hall of Fame* special. The girl I played opposite had something like four pages of dialogue and I only just had reaction shots. She'd say all her lines and finally my line would be, "I understand," and then she'd have another four pages of dialogue. I was a great reactor and started getting all those kinds of parts. It was my niche. Time went on, and one day there was this audition for the first television pilot of *Happy Days*. I was one of the last people out of hundreds to audition, but I got the part. However, the original pilot didn't sell, and I went back to doing boyfriend parts. That was around 1972.

About a year later, the movie *American Graffiti* came out and was a big hit. ABC said, "Didn't we do a pilot of something like this?" They called us all back. This time I went in with my actor friend Ron Howard, but because we were older now, he was eighteen, I was twenty-three. We had to do a screen test along with a number of other really talented competitors. Ron and I went in together and talked to them together. They set us up to do the test the next morning, and we would be the first up. Ron was more experienced than me, but I was more of an entrepreneurial-type guy and told Ron, "Wouldn't it be kind of cool if we came in with some ideas for the show?"

"Yeah," he said. "Usually the test is pretty quick. You just say some lines and leave."

"Why don't we sneak on the set early and block ourselves and then act like it's all spontaneous?"

"Great idea," Ron said. So we found out where the shoot was going to be, and we rehearsed for a couple hours. Then, the next morning when the director was there, we were coming up with all these planned ideas. And the director spent two hours with us instead of twenty minutes like he did the others. We got the parts together, and *Happy Days* became a major prime-time hit.

The three main high school characters were Fonzie (Henry Winkler), Richie (Ron Howard), and Potsie (me). Originally, the show was written as Richie Cunningham being the main character. But the numbers weren't that great, so the producers suggested that the show change and be written around Fonzie as the main character. Ron Howard was so cool about it and totally humbled himself, and that change made all the difference. By the end of the third season, we were number one in the world and the cast members were household names. Something I learned from Ron Howard is: to be really successful in life you have to be somewhat selfless. That's what made *Happy Days* work.

For the next five years I couldn't go anywhere without security. It was crazy, but I lived very conservatively. I had an apartment and then bought a little house. What helped me stay grounded was that I understood my place on the show. I realized that I was never going to be *the* main character but always in a supporting role. It's a good place, but I knew it wouldn't last forever. Being the entrepreneurial spirit that I am I also knew I had to take advantage of the opportunity and create something out of it. Because I loved to sing, my first creative idea was to have a live band on the show. You know, one of those garage-type high school bands. Again, I was thinking out-side the box and presented it to Garry Marshall. I figured what did I have to lose? The worst he could say was no. Well, he didn't say no, thought it was a great idea, and told me that he'd give it a shot. The first episode went well, and Garry said he'd put the band in every few shows. The condition was that I had to be responsible for coming up with the songs, the rehearsing, and the production.

Now, instead of just having my acting part, I was in charge of producing and coming up with the music that I'd be singing on the show. I relished the challenge, and the band became a hit. Because of the great response, it got my entrepreneurial mind churning up other possibilities. I started thinking record contract and concerts. To sum it up, I wound up doing concerts on the weekends earning ten times what I was making per week on the show. You read correctly. I was earning ten times at con-certs what I was earning each week on *Happy Days*. Because I was singing on the show I had worldwide visibility and could get booked for a concert whenever I wanted. Of course, I had to work harder because I didn't have a natural voice that could just belt out incredible vocals, but I could sing and play catchy tunes. Bottom line: 30,000 people were coming to my concerts. It was nuts. I saw an opportunity and took it. It was all about being entrepreneurial. I created it. Instead of thinking, *Oh God, I'm not the star of the show,* I thought, *What are my possibilities? What can I do to better myself? What is a healthy opportunity?* I had to get rid of my ego.

Happy Days had a great run but ended in 1984, and so did the concerts. Because of my fame, after the show ended I was getting booked in hotels and casinos to sing as a co-headliner in the main rooms, but I could see the handwriting on the wall. I knew that the next stop would be the lounges if I didn't have the strength to change direction. I had never sung in the lounges and knew that I didn't want to wind up doing that for the rest of my life. I tried not to have an unrealistic look at myself. Don't ever let your ego or small-mindedness get in the way. Get outside of it. I knew I had to reinvent myself yet again. That's when I went fully behind the camera.

The first show that I created and sold was coproduced and directed with Ron Howard. It was a TV movie titled *Skyward* with Bette Davis. One day I had this idea for an original story and pitched it to Ron. We sold it to NBC, but they told us we needed to get someone like a Bette Davis. Getting someone of her caliber to act in my first little movie seemed next to impossible, but we went for it and she said yes! Since then, I've directed at least 200 episodes for television, including *Melrose Place; Beverly Hills, 90210; Star Trek: Voyager; Star Trek: Deep Space Nine; Sabrina, the Teenage Witch;* and *Charmed.*

In my life I've always had success when I took action on my own instead of waiting for someone else to make the decisions. I've always been entrepreneurial and looked for opportunity. When doing *Melrose Place* I met JoAnna Connell, a woman who was a well-respected makeup artist and also a product developer for the film industry. She had created all the skin-care products for *Baywatch,* and created their beautiful tans. In addition to that, JoAnna created a phenomenal skin treatment she was using on the actors. The cast began raving about these products. A light went off in my head and I saw an opportunity. Literally that day, I went into her trailer and convinced her to create a business together. I told JoAnna, "I'll figure out how to present it and sell it. You create it." This wasn't impulsive, rather it was intuitive. I've just always had an innate sense for marketing.

Because the products were already being used in the television business, we had a solid base of guaranteed sales. While we were not getting rich, that sales base gave us the ability to learn mass manufacturing on a small scale and never go in the red. We did small runs and never had inventory issues. We made a lot of mistakes, but we were learning the business. Selling to just the entertainment industry didn't make us that much money because it's not a mass market. Deep down, I just knew the business had huge potential if we could expand outside the industry.

During this time, because of a number of factors—the economy and the ups and downs of show business—I started getting fewer and fewer directing opportunities. I was never out of work as a director, I just got fewer offers. It was a very scary time, and my gut told me to jump into the skin-care product business full time. My gut said, "Do it," but everybody else thought I was absolutely crazy. I made the commitment to go full throttle, which meant sacrificing some of my directing. My wife and friends all thought I was utterly insane.

What made the whole thing seem even more insane was that I started working the business at swap meets, which is a glorified flea market. I actually turned down directing offers to work at the swap meet. I knew this choice was a risk, but again, my gut told me to take it for greater opportunities. For almost a year on Thursdays, Fridays, Saturdays, and Sundays, we worked the indoor swap meet at Woodland Hills to try and figure out what worked and what didn't work, what people liked and what they didn't like. On Thursdays, I'd go in myself and mop up the booth and make it clean for Friday. We were giving away the products so people could give us feedback and we could do marketing research. We weren't making any money, but we got thousands of people on lists. It was humbling, but I learned the business really well and just had this gut feeling that it was going in the right direction, that all of this was going to pay off. I was learning what attracted people, what got them excited, and what turned them off. All those were tools we needed. That swap meet was better than going to Yale School of Management.

After we spent about a year doing our homework, we began our marketing and started doing very well. We got a rep that went around pushing our products, which led us to our QVC connection and also started building our retail sales. The name of our main company is StarMaker Products. Now we've started a second company, Physicians Prefer (www.physiciansprefer.com). We financed a group of doctors, clinical pharmacists, and chemists who are committed to creating products that are clinically proven and 100 percent drug free for use in relieving debilitating conditions. One of our amazing products is a little topical gel with no hormones, no estrogen, and no drugs that is 100 percent clinically proven to relieve hot flashes. It's called Cool Flash for the Hot Flash and is now backed by Dr. Ernie Bodai, the creator of the Breast Cancer Research Stamp, and is used on thousands of chemo patients to relieve them of flashes caused by the procedure. A percentage of every sale goes to www.curebreastcancer.org.

Ten years ago, I knew nothing about the skin-care business. At the end of *Happy Days* I could have stopped at that and gone around doing autograph shows and things like that. And that would have been okay, but that wasn't me. I refused to be defined by people telling me who or what I am, trying to keep me in their box. I'm all about stepping outside the boxes. For me, *Happy Days* was just an opportunity to do other things. It was just a start, not an end. The interesting thing is, the minute the skin-care business started really taking off I got a couple of directing offers, and that whole thing came back full circle. Today I co-own two multimillion-dollar companies, and I'm busier than I've ever been as a director. Currently, I'm one of the two alternating directors on the hit show *The Secret Life of the American Teenager*. Never stop looking for possibilities and opportunities for reinvention, because you never know which one is going to succeed or which is going to fail, or if both will succeed!

To learn more about Anson Williams and StarMaker Products, check out www.Starmakerproducts.com.

Creating Opportunities

◆

DeLando Brass—Successful Business Owner of Paradise Smoothie

"We often miss opportunity because it's dressed
in overalls and looks like work."

—Thomas A. Edison

Growing up as a black kid in the early 1970s was tough, especially because my father was never around and my mom was single trying to raise me and my two sisters on her own while trying to attend nursing school. I can remember many, many days when the refrigerator was empty and the electricity had been turned off. As a result, when other kids were playing ball and doing kid stuff, I went to work doing what I knew I could do, mowing lawns. I just had an old push mower, nothing self-propelled, but I was gifted to be able to knock on people's doors and say, "Hey, my name is Del. Would you like your yard mowed?" Fortunately, many of the adults and parents in our neighborhood held me in pretty high regard as a little black kid, and after a short time I had built up a huge clientele. I had clients both black and white (mostly white) that trusted me to do their lawns even when they were out of town. In the fall, I doubled down. I'd mulch leaves, but would also take out trash and do other chores that needed to be done. I made sure my clients' trash was out by the street. After the trash man had picked up, I'd go back and collect the cans. If animals had gotten into the trash, I'd clean it up. During my middle school years, it got to the point where I was making an easy $125 a week. The money that I made I took home to Mom and my two sisters. Because they were girls, they always had greater needs than me, like dresses, shoes, makeup, and that kind of stuff. I would give them money to get what they needed. My mind-set was that I was always contributing to the needs of the household.

Then, when I was in the seventh grade, my mother had a heart attack one day while she was working as a nurse. I was told outside her room in intensive care, "You should probably prepare yourself because your mom is not going to see you out of middle school." She was diagnosed with coronary artery spasms with seizure and was sick for an extended period, which made it difficult for her to hold down a consistent job.

All my buddies were into sports, and I wanted to play in the worst way, but couldn't because I had to work the lawn service or whatever I could get to keep things going. My grades were excellent, and I always stayed in school. Something I must say is we were getting very little government assistance. My oldest sister, who was well into high school, was getting just twelve dollars a month from the government, while my other sister and I each got much less per month. For the longest time, my mother would send the government checks back! However, we did get food stamps, and that was tough for me. I was too prideful to spend them. If I absolutely had to go to the store to spend the food stamps, I'd drive somewhere that I was sure nobody knew me.

Because my mother was so ill, at fourteen I was driving all over the city without a driver's license, paying bills, and taking care of the household business. I'd drive to the electric company on the last day to pay before they cut us off and things like that. By God's grace, I never got stopped by the police, not one time.

One day in the eighth grade, my best white friend, Tony Busby, was getting picked on by a bunch of guys, and I took up for him. I mean I plowed the road for him. Afterward, he invited me to his house for the first time. When I got there I couldn't believe people actually lived like that. I mean, he had all the best toys and games and the refrigerator was crammed full of food. I'd never seen so much food. It was like taking me to the candy store! And Mr. and Mrs. Busby were like, "Now Del, you don't have to ask for anything. You just get whatever you want. If you want something, you just jerk that refrigerator door open and you get it. You just make yourself at home." And they meant it.

Mr. Busby owned a roofing company and knew about my situation. He told me if I wanted a job he'd hire me to work each day after school. So after school I'd run home, get changed, and run over to Mr. Busby's house, and someone would always be there to pick me up and take me to wherever the crew was working. Usually, it was Tony's older brother, Timmy.

I started carrying bundles of shingles on my shoulders from the truck to the ladder and lift. When the roofers would tear off shingles and throw them down, I'd pick them up and put them in a container or roll the magnetic bar to pick up the nails. I did whatever they told me, and finally they let me go on the roof and taught me how to tear off the shingles. So I'd tear off shingles, throw them to the ground, and go down and pick them up. I did it and never complained. Mr. Busby paid me $200 a week and I was still in middle school! I know it was excessive, but I saw it as God's provision. I worked for Mr. Busby until I was in high school and he moved away to another city.

A group of about fifteen of us neighborhood kids always walked to school. Once, for several days, while walking to school, we passed a man who was probably in his thirties. His name was Mr. Dupard and he would just watch us and wave. After a few days he said, "Hey, you young men, come here." We walked over and he said, "I do carpentry work, and I have so much work that I need help." He asked for our names and phone numbers and wrote them down in his notebook. I didn't find this out until later, but I was the only one he called. He said, "I watched your group every morning walking to school. I was listening and observing. I heard what was being said. When you spoke to me, young man, you made eye contact and you weren't shuffling around." He hired me. God had provided work for me yet again, and this time I started learning woodworking and cabinetry. Eventually, he taught me how to build and install cabinets. During high school, he just kept me busy, out of trouble, and paid me well.

Finally, I made it out of high school and to college. During that time, I started working at night as a security officer for a condominium development. I did that for a while then took a year off from college to travel the country working as a counselor for VisionQuest International, an alternative program for troubled inner-city youth. They were a co-op company, which meant because the job was within my major I got paid and received college credit. It was a life-changing experience for me. When I returned to school I went back to the condominium development where I had previously worked and talked to the lady who was the director of the association. She said, "You have no idea how much I've missed you. I want you back."

I said, "Well, I came by to see if you could give me a letter of referral that I could take back to the security company I worked for and see if they will rehire me."

"I don't want that company," she said. "I want you."

"Are you going to hire another company?" I said.

"You'll be the company," she said. "I'll give you these condominiums as your first security account."

So I started looking into what it would take to open my own security-officer business. I went downtown and checked on all of the fees and licensing requirements. I went back to her and explained that it would be so expensive that I would never be able to do all this, that I needed several thousand dollars to set up my company, get registered with the state, licensed, pay other fees, and get equipment. Her response was, "You come to the board meeting on Monday night. We're going to talk to the board members and we are going to loan you that money so you can get started. How much monthly salary do you need?" I threw out what I thought was a fair figure based on what other companies were paying, and because I was engaged to be married at the time, she doubled it!

I went to that board meeting and they loaned me the money. I got all the requirements met and went to work as the owner of my own, very small, one-person security company. But more than that, I saw an opportunity for something bigger and seized it. I learned how to replicate myself and eventually had 150 employees working for me. We provided security for condominiums, restaurants, supermarkets, and other establishments all across the state and brought in $4.5 million my best year.

Now, I have to tell you, it wasn't all peaches and cream. There was one point when the company was growing but I kept hitting roadblocks. I was getting the door slammed in my face, and for the first time I felt it was because of my race. I even went in for counsel with my pastor, Raymond W. Johnson, and told him that there were certain obstacles that I just couldn't get past because I was black and I was thinking about giving up. He said, "If you think you can't succeed because you're black, then you're a failure because God is no respecter of persons and wants you to succeed."

I didn't quit, but I took an unfortunate shortcut on God's plan of slower, patient growth. Instead of being patient, I let my pride and ambition get the best of me. There was a white guy working as a salesman for the security company I used to work for. He was one of their top salesmen and could sell anything to anybody. He came to see me one day and said, "My life is falling apart. I've got a good job making lots of money. But I'm not happy. My wife's not happy. I'm drinking, and that's the last thing I need to be doing. I want to make a change. I want to start over. I'm asking you for an opportunity to work with you to help your business grow and also to help myself change."

I told him I would pay him a certain salary but after each new account that he closed, I'd give him a bonus. His response was, "Oh man. This is great! Thank you!" The first challenge I gave him was a really hard account that I'd been trying to close. It was a guy who needed security services but was slamming the door in my face because I was black. Within a few days, my new salesman had closed that account. After that, he started closing accounts left and right. His pay was going up. My pay was going up. The business was exploding. I went from a small, obscure company to one where I was being approached by big conglomerates who wanted to buy me out and give me a job! But I refused to sell, and we just kept growing.

Suddenly, when it seemed my life was finally coming together, I fell ill with a strange sickness. My tongue swelled until I could barely talk. My ears closed so that I could barely hear. My hands and feet swelled, and I couldn't walk. I couldn't even put on socks. It was bad. This happened right after the first Gulf War, and I had been in the National Guard. My unit hadn't been deployed, but I did come into contact with personnel returning from the war. Doctors ran all kinds of tests and never could figure out exactly what it was, but concluded it might be Gulf War syndrome.

I was out of commission for three weeks and got better. But I got sick again and this time was down for three months. During those months my partner went wild. Behind my back, he started a business of his own. He'd solicit potential clients. Then he'd pay his people through my payroll account. I was doing paperwork from home, but I had no clue what was going on. He was running his employees through my payroll. On top of that, he had many fictitious, phantom employees who were working for him at different fictitious companies. Checks were made out to these fictitious people, and he co-endorsed them for the money. After disputes arose with disgruntled employees, they complained to the Regulatory Commission, so I was compelled to submit documents for an audit of my company. It was then that I realized that many things were wrong!

Eventually, my former partner came to me and admitted that what he did was wrong. He broke down and started weeping, telling me that he had some real problems and that he'd gotten off base. When it was all said and done, he asked for my forgiveness. Forgiving him was the last thing I wanted to do. I'm not going to say what I felt like doing. Yet, at that moment a light came on in my mind and an inner voice said to me, "Del, everything that you are is predicated on the fact that you first received forgiveness for your transgressions. We all have transgressions we need God's forgiveness for. Now you have to forgive him." And I did. I really forgave him. But the business was finished, and I hit rock bottom.

Even though I had forgiven my former partner, I was angry because he was able to move on. He actually went to jail for a short time, but I couldn't get past my monumental failure. For several years I just spun my wheels struggling to reinvent myself, to find my niche. I knew the right opportunity was out there, I just had to find it.

One day I stopped in a Paradise Smoothie store to get a drink. Paradise Smoothie is a chain of smoothie stores similar to Smoothie King. It just so happened that the founder was there and was talking to some guys about problems he was having with the construction of one of his new stores. His contractor had quit, leaving him in a bind. I overheard and walked up to him and said, "Hey, I understand you're having some problems. I can do what you need to have done."

"Is that so?" he asked, and we set up a time to meet at his other store.

I walked into that store, which was basically a shell, and said, "Man, most of your electrical and plumbing is done. All you need is the finishing on it—floors and ceilings and paint. I can finish this in fifteen days."

"Fifteen days?" He looked surprised.

"That's right," I said, and we made an agreement on the spot. I rallied a group of jack-of-all-trade guys I'd known through the years, and we finished that store in nine days. The owner was thrilled, and after that he asked me to help with another project, and we knocked that one out fast, too.

One day I asked him, "Hey man, how can I get involved in the Paradise Smoothie business?"

"If you help me with another project," he said, "I'll get you started."

I finished some other stores, and he helped me learn the business. For about a year, I reinvented myself, learning how to run the cash register, how to make smoothies, how to operate a Paradise Smoothie store. And I wasn't being paid. Now I'm a successful owner of one Paradise Smoothie store and am planning to open another three in the next eighteen months. I couldn't be happier.

Opportunities are out there for everybody, regardless of their race or economic status. Even the downtimes can spur you on to success. I was handed several opportunities—to mow lawns, roof houses, build cabinets, start a security company, hit rock bottom, help a man get out of a bind, and then reinvent myself as a Paradise Smoothie store owner. I simply had to put myself in a position to find these opportunities and be willing to roll up my sleeves and work to take advantage of the open doors. It can work that way for all of us.

DeLando owns Paradise Smoothie in Central City outside of Baton Rouge, Louisiana.

In the Face of Skeptics

◆

Mary Kay Ash—Founder of Mary Kay Cosmetics and Women's Rights Advocate

"Aerodynamics have proven that the bumblebee
cannot fly. The body is too heavy and the
wings are too weak. But the bumblebee doesn't know
that, and it goes right on flying, miraculously."

—Mary Kay Ash

An important note about all the do-over stories in this book, including the American Classics, is that each one is about an average person just like you and me, from mundane backgrounds, facing incredible obstacles. Yet, refusing to wear the cloak of victim or to be chained down by circumstances, they forged forward and wound up doing extraordinary things. Mary Kay Ash is no exception. She was born in 1918 to average parents who ran a restaurant and inn in the small town of Hot Wells, Texas. Then, in the early 1920s, her father became bedridden with tuberculosis. To support the family, her mother worked at a restaurant twenty-five miles away in Houston, leaving the responsibility of caring for her father and running the family's household square on Mary Kay's seven-year-old shoulders.

With the responsibilities of an adult thrust upon her, Mary Kay was forced to grow up fast. "If I needed new clothing," she recalled, "I had to go by myself to downtown Houston. I took these Saturday trips alone, because my best friend was not allowed to travel on the streetcar without an adult. After all, we were just seven years old."

Mary Kay had always been a superior student with a lot of drive and determination. Despite the pressures from home, she loved school and made straight As, graduating from high school in just three years. Yet, her dreams of college would have to be delayed for lack of money. This was before the days of financial aid like we have available for students today. On top of that, because of the bad economy brought on by the Great Depression, jobs were scarce, even for someone with Mary Kay's abilities.

In 1930, at the age of seventeen, she married and had three children within seven years. But after her husband went into World War II, she was forced to go to work to help support her family. But again, because of the Depression-era economy, her options were severely limited. It was during this time, however, that a woman knocked on Mary Kay's front door, selling children's books. Mary Kay liked the books but couldn't afford them. The saleswoman told her, "If you can sell ten sets, you'll get a set free." Always up for a challenge, Mary Kay sold the ten sets in less than two days, and over the next several months sold more than

$25,000 worth of books! It was a great victory for Mary Kay and a boost to her self-esteem. But then, life turned bitter again.

As soon as her husband returned from the war, he divorced her and abandoned the family, leaving Mary Kay as the sole financial support for her three children. "I had developed a sense of worth for my abilities as a wife and mother, [I knew I was a good salesperson], and yet on that day I felt like a complete failure." After the divorce, she fell back on what she knew she could do—sales. She went to work for Stanley Home Products, a direct sales firm out of Houston.

Over the next twenty years, Mary Kay worked as a salesperson for Stanley Home Products and then eventually for the World Gift Company. Then, in 1960 she married a Dallas businessman named George Hallenbeck. With her personal life soaring, Mary Kay's sales also soared, but despite her success, in 1963, her male assistant, whom she had personally trained, was promoted to a position above her. It was the worst in a string of inequities she'd experienced at the company because she was a woman. "I was constantly being told, 'Oh, Mary Kay, you're thinking female.' And inevitably, no matter how hard I tried, no matter how well I did my job, I still found myself reaching the golden door only to find it marked 'Men Only.'"

At the age of forty-five Mary Kay found herself unemployed. With the children grown and her out of work, she felt pretty worthless and slipped into deep depression. To combat the depression, Mary Kay began journaling all the things she had done well and the obstacles she had overcome. As she was writing, it occurred to her to turn the journal into a book that would emphasize her twenty-five years of direct-sales wisdom. Part of the manuscript included the plans for starting and building a "dream company." The more she studied the idea and wrote about it, another thing occurred to her. *Instead of writing about the dream company,* she thought to herself, *why don't I just start one?*

Mary Kay had discovered a potential line of skin-care and makeup products that she believed in and felt she could market. But her most impressive innovation was her sales approach. Her idea was to use the house-party sales method pioneered by Tupperware to reach customers on a person-to-person level by doing personal makeovers for women in their homes. Hers would also be a company built with the specific needs and challenges of women employees in mind, like offering flexibility to part-time workers so they could be committed to their families while still making an income. Although making money was important, Mary Kay had a higher agenda, to offer women opportunities that never before existed.

Of course, the skeptics mocked her idea and model. Still, in 1963, undaunted, in the face of her skeptics, Mary Kay and her husband, George, pulled their life savings of $5,000 out of the bank and started their company, Beauty by Mary Kay. The money was used to produce a small inventory and lease a 500-square-foot storefront. Mary Kay would recruit the first set of consultants, while George handled the finances. Together, the couple worked at night labeling and boxing the products.

Then, just a couple weeks before the planned grand opening of the company, tragedy hit Mary Kay's life once more. While eating breakfast, George Hallenbeck suffered a massive heart attack and died at the kitchen table. Alone again, Mary Kay felt herself sliding back into despair—a place she knew she couldn't go to again and survive. So she avoided a breakdown by immersing herself in her work. Mary Kay's attorney strongly discouraged her from moving forward and showed her documented statistics on the high failure rate of new business start-ups. Going against his advice, Mary Kay forged ahead with her dream. Her son, Ben Rogers, came to her aid, contributing an additional $4,500 from his personal savings account.

Because of her cunning business tactics, Mary Kay didn't require much start-up capital, and from 1963 to 1978, her company grew at a phenomenal average annual rate of 28 percent. In 1976, Mary Kay Cosmetics became the first company headed by a woman to be listed on the New York Stock Exchange. Today, Mary Kay Cosmetics continues to inspire and instill self-esteem in women around the world, all because Mary Kay took the initiative to reinvent her life.

Sources

Ash, Mary Kay. *Mary Kay.* New York: Harper & Row, 1981.

Ash, Mary Kay. *Mary Kay on People Management.* New York: Warner Books, 1984.

Gove, John. *Made in America: The True Stories Behind the Brand Names that Built a Nation.* New York: Berkley, 2001.

Gross, Daniel. *Forbes: Greatest Business Stories of All Time.* New York: John Wiley & Sons, 1996.

My "Inner Voice"

◆

Edna Valentino—Female Bodybuilder, Personal Trainer, and Life Coach

"Trust your hunches. They're usually based on facts
filed away just below the conscious level."

—Joyce Brothers

"At this time we do not have any openings in the department to which you inquire. Should something become available we will contact you. Thank you." It was such a letdown. Twice in the last six months I had received this rejection letter from the one network I was dying to work for. A couple of years earlier, I had graduated with a bachelor of arts degree in mass communications and a concentration in television production. After college, I took a job at a local television station in Pennsylvania. It was a full-time position as a camera operator and technical director in the control room. I learned a lot really quickly. After about six months, I was competent at my job but soon became bored. The "voice" in my head told me, *go where you can grow!*

I was determined to get my résumé in as many hands as possible. I asked for referrals, and I applied for work everywhere. I looked online. I read the classifieds in the back of trade magazines. I even sent my résumé to everyone under the "video production" category in the phone book!

But all along I was drawn to that station that had turned me down twice. It had a great reputation. It was big. It was local, and it was very hard to get into. I had always heard that it was difficult even to get an interview at the network if you didn't know someone who worked there, and I didn't. But I wasn't about to give up, and as luck would have it, I found someone who could help me. A gentleman who owned his own wedding video business had received one of my résumés. He told me that he didn't have a job for me at his company but that he knew someone at the big network who did. I was flabbergasted! This perfect stranger received my résumé, didn't have a job for me, but still picked up the phone and gave me a referral. He could have just as easily tossed my résumé in the trash and moved on with his day, but he took a close look at it instead. I was grateful for his act of kindness that put my résumé in front of the network for the third and pivotal time.

A couple of weeks later, my future boss asked me to come in for an interview. When I walked into the massive building, it was love at first sight. I remember at the interview thinking, *I could see myself working at this company for at least five years.* At that age, five years was a lifetime! The longest job I had ever held up until that point lasted just two years. In the end, I was at the big network for eight.

Working there was absolutely riveting! What was most impressive was that the network offered twenty-four hours of live television. The studio buzzed with excitement! Many of the employees were young people just out of college like me, so they brought with them a lively energy that was a perfect match for this live-show environment. The network had a reputation for promoting from within, so that's why it was so difficult to get a job from the outside. I found that many of my coworkers had been working at the company for more than fifteen years. Many had worked their way up from low man on the totem pole to their current roles as manager, director, and even vice president. I was looking forward to a long future at my new home. But since I was just starting out, I was working crazy hours, including the graveyard shift, or, "the yard," as we called it. Although I loved my job, I needed something more. *What kind of hobbies were out there for me so that I could have a life outside of work?*

Growing up, I'd always played team sports, so I joined a gym to stay active. At twenty-three years old, I purchased my very first gym membership. As a gym "newbie," I remember being so nervous about walking into the weight room that for several months I only did the cardio machines. The only reason I didn't get bored was because of all the fitness magazines I read. They featured women doing bodybuilding and fitness competitions. Bodybuilding was about getting as muscular and lean as possible, and the women posed on stage barefoot. The women in fitness didn't have to be as lean; plus, they posed on stage in five-inch heels and were judged on a two-minute fitness routine while they wore a costume. Many times I found myself engrossed in the pictures of the competitors dancing and tumbling. They were like acrobats flying through the air. I imagined it to be such a rush!

I adopted their mind-set. Many women used visualization techniques in conjunction with training methods and nutrition plans that allowed them to compete at the highest levels. Eventually, I couldn't take it anymore. Reading the articles and looking at the pictures was no longer enough. I just had to compete myself!

After a conversation with my husband, who was the foundation of my support system, I decided that I would learn the basics of the trade and start with a bodybuilding show. This would provide me with a chance to learn how to train, how to eat, and how to prioritize my life while still working my crazy schedule at the network. Ultimately, I aspired to compete in a fitness competition where I could wear my five-inch heels followed by my two-minute routine. That was my vision!

It took me a few weeks to get into a solid workout routine. Once established, I trained hard six days a week. Some days I was motivated. Other days my commitment and discipline were tested. Usually, those were the days I had worked through the night and was starting my workout already fatigued. Those mornings were rough.

I remember working out alone one day and trying to motivate myself to do some hill sprints after a killer leg workout. The hill wasn't all that big, but when you are absolutely exhausted any slight incline can conjure an image of Mount Everest. I kept talking to myself to keep me focused. *What's it going to take, Edna? Are you up for the challenge?* As I reached the most intense point of the hill, I finally asked myself, *How badly do you want it?* That last question resonated with me more than any other self-talk I had tried. And in that moment, that question became my mantra. I held on to the words and carried them with me to every workout and to every social event where I might be tempted to stray from my diet plan. When the going got rough, I asked myself that question. Sometimes the answer was "not badly enough right now," and I'd let myself off the hook. Maybe I needed to get to bed and sleep first. Maybe I needed a day off all together. Other days, my mantra was the trigger that got me back on track and kept me focused on the competition.

To this day, I use my mantra in any situation I find challenging. In fact, many of my friends have used this question to get through their long-distance runs, bike rides, and challenging workouts. You might try it! It's quite powerful. Seven months later, it was time to compete. I felt as prepared as I could possibly be. My mother and my friends were out in the audience ready to cheer me on. I also had my workout partner, Susan, or as I called her "my backbone," with me backstage. She was there for me from day one. Susan was so dedicated to helping me fulfill my goal that she would pack my meals the few times I traveled for work. When I went on vacation, she would draw up workout programs for me to take. She was always there when I needed inspiration.

My sister helped me keep my nerves down on the ninety-minute ride to the competition. I could hear her in the audience shouting my name the whole time I was on stage. And a couple of other veteran competitors were backstage as part of my entourage as well. They helped me get my swimsuit glued in the right places, made sure my tanner was evenly applied, and greased me up for the bright lights on stage. I had always believed in the importance of having a strong support system, but never before had I seen its full power in my life. Surrounding myself with people who were selfless with their time and energy was imperative. I had no chance of getting through this journey without my team.

That night I won my first bodybuilding competition! I will never forget the overwhelming feeling of wonder as I stood on that stage accepting my trophy. If you could draw a picture of what I was feeling, it would look like ripples of energy emanating from all over my body! Listening to my intuition, defining my vision, creating my mantra, and assembling my support system, plus passion and plain hard work, had led me to this nirvana. I knew in that moment that I wanted every woman to feel exactly what I was feeling—that no matter how lofty the goal may seem, you can do absolutely *anything* you set your mind to do! After that pivotal day, I knew that I needed to act on that certainty and soon determined that the best way to communicate that message to others was by getting my personal training certification.

So later that year, I earned my certification through the American Council on Exercise. My old gym owner hired me part time at his personal training studio while I continued to work full time at the network. I trained anyone and everyone I could get my hands on. I found the work absolutely rewarding!

Six months later I found myself facing a dilemma. I either had to reduce the number of clients I trained or quit my full-time job. I noticed that I wasn't able to do both at the same time very well. The hard part was that I loved the work I was doing in each position. I had worked at the network for eight years and was very comfortable. Everything was live and exciting! My coworkers created a wonderful work environment, and I knew without a doubt that I could have worked my way up the corporate ladder and had a long, healthy career there. On the other hand, I loved inspiring people on a one-on-one level. I knew that I was changing women's lives by helping them feel confident in their bodies through personal training. In my own experience, I felt my most powerful when I was secure in my physical body. I loved being able to support women in making that same connection.

It was an extremely difficult decision that I mulled over for weeks. *Would I regret leaving my "comfort zone" at the network? Would I be able to pay the bills on a personal trainer's salary?* Finally, I realized that as much as I loved working at the network, I was finding a sense of fulfillment as a personal trainer that I wasn't finding elsewhere. Two weeks later, I officially became a full-time personal trainer. I couldn't believe that I had actually quit my "day job" to follow a passion that had blossomed only in the last few years.

This passion for fitness led me down a road with many unexpected turns. By remaining open not only to my "inner voice" but the voices and experiences of my clients, my career path has continued to evolve. An experience with one personal-training client in particular led to an awakening that losing weight is about much more than diet and exercise. I saw that by dealing with the dissatisfaction in our lives, in conjunction with working out and eating right, we can lose weight more easily—which led to my exploring the world of life coaching. Ultimately, I opened a business that uniquely combines personal training and life coaching. To this day, I see the combined approaches helping my clients achieve success more quickly and effectively.

In the end, I believe that every career reinvention or "do over" has been a part of my personal evolution. I have stayed open and listened for my inner voice to move me onto the next phase of my journey. As a result, I have been invested in but never permanently attached to anything I have been doing. Although it may sound surprising, I actually have enjoyed the risks I've taken. They've made life more exciting. And since listening to my intuition has guided my steps, I have already felt successful along the way, which, in turn, has made each transition feel more comfortable. Yes, there has been doubt sometimes, maybe even fear, but there has also been trust.

Trusting my intuition has been the best part of these do overs! Why? Because I am having so much fun doing things that motivate people to be their best selves. I believe that when you feel good in both your mind and body, you show up in the world differently. So, today I am a life coach and personal trainer . . . for now. . . .

Edna Valentino is a life coach and personal trainer. You can visit her at www.AwakeningsLifeCoach.com or www.EdnaValentino.com.

Love Me Do Over

♦

Rick Domeier—
Husband, Father, and QVC Program Host

"When I met you, no heart knew me.
When I met you, romance picked me up and threw me
Through the wondrous moonlit sky, landing next to you.
An angel wrote this song, when I met you."

—Richard George

"Oh yah," my cousin Tom said in his thickest Minnesota accent. "Nice night."

"Yah, not too humid," I said, jumping into Minnesota-speak myself.

"Geez, I think it might be time for another beer," he said. "You in?"

"Oh yah, you betcha."

The fact is, it was hard *not* to fall back into a Minnesota accent. This was home. We were in the midst of a huge crowd. It was Heritagefest, a German American celebration that took place every year in my hometown of New Ulm. Huge tents covered the entire fairgrounds. The tents were filled with polka bands from Munich, polka dancing, laughter, bratwurst, sauerkraut, and oh yah, a beer or two. It's one of the few places where you don't think twice about seeing a guy wearing lederhosen. It was a gathering place for people of all ages, including lots of college-age kids home for the summer. Tom and I were both back for our ten-year high school reunion. Tom was happily married with kids. I was single. As we made our way from one tent to another, we ran into old friends and reminisced. I was in the middle of one of those "Remember that one time" stories when I looked to my left. I saw a beautiful girl with blonde hair, Scandinavian features, and gorgeous green eyes. She couldn't have been more than twenty years old. She glanced over and quickly looked away. Cousin Tom caught me staring.

"Beautiful. But too young," he said. "You don't stand a chance."

I managed to find the courage to stumble over and say hello, dragging Tom with me. She was surrounded by other girlfriends. "My name's Rick," I said, suddenly feeling confident and mature.

"My name's Amy," she said. "So, how *old* are you guys, anyway?"

After the group laughter died down, I was able to clarify my ancient age of twenty-eight, the ten-year high school reunion, and the fact that any day now, I would be getting my AARP card in the mail. She was bright, pretty, funny, and to top it off, really nice. Minnesota nice. I was smitten. I was a smitten old man.

As the night's festivities came to a close, I asked her out on a good old-fashioned, small-town date. The next night at dinner, we laughed like high school kids, which, for her age, wasn't much of a stretch. We talked about how different our lives were, her college life at St. Cloud State, and how much she loved riding horses with her father. I tried way too hard to make my life in Los Angeles seem more glamorous than it actually was. We exchanged a kiss (okay, several kisses, but don't tell her dad)!

I came home that night and told my mom, "This is the sweetest person I've ever met. Now that's the kind of girl I'd like to marry."

"It's about time," she said.

My buddy Dean and I left on a rock-climbing adventure the next day. For the life of me, I couldn't stop thinking about this girl. I called Amy from a pay phone in Rapid City (yes, a pay phone). We talked. I was completely infatuated. Dean and I set out to climb Devil's Tower in Wyoming. Looking at the extraordinary mountain jutting out from the earth, we had originally planned to climb one side, but decided to take a different route. Sort of like my career, my relationships, and my life in L.A.

♦ ♦ ♦ ♦

Back in the late eighties, Los Angeles, California, was a place where big dreams and brutal realities came crashing into one another like BMWs on the Hollywood Freeway. It was a combination of elation, rejection, success, and absurd contradictions. It was an intoxicating cocktail. I ordered a double. Looking back today, I sometimes gasp for air and wonder, "How did I survive?" One hot summer night, in the middle of a busy intersection in Los Alamitos, a big, mean SUV smashed into the passenger side of my friendly little Honda. I walked away, but it was good-bye Honda. On another occasion, I was held up at gunpoint outside the infamous Frolic Room on Hollywood Boulevard. Yet another night, at 2:00 AM in downtown L.A., I was sitting in my car at a red light. Two speeding cars filled with rival gang members flew past me, doing eighty-five mph. Shots were firing the entire time. It all happened in the span of five seconds. When the light turned green, I just sat there, my fingers frozen to the steering wheel. Note to self: avoid downtown L.A. at two o'clock in the morning.

But other aspects of life in L.A. were equally fascinating—only in a good way. After receiving a scholarship to study at the Tony Award–winning South Coast Repertory, I was exposed to great theater training and had the opportunity to work with wonderfully talented, sometimes crazy people. Studying the Stanislavsky technique was like entering another world. I joined other actors and directors to form a theater troupe called Genesis Company. With very little money, we were the actors, the set builders, and (in the old days before e-mail campaigns) even the guys who placed flyers in car windows. I had the opportunity to perform Shakespeare, Arthur Miller, David Mamet, and more. I lived in an apartment with my roommates, Jeff and Mike. It was not exactly upscale. Okay, it was a total dive. Had we planted seeds into the dirt of the bathtub ring, we could have grown corn. Those were the starving-artist days. Which was great, except for, you know, the starving part. During the entire time, I dated, yet remained single—very single. Settling down? Starting a family? You gotta be kidding me. I have an audition tomorrow!

I remember auditioning on the Columbia Pictures lot for the first time (five lines as a cop on *Days of Our Lives*). There was the moment I got my SAG (Screen Actors Guild) card, I was a mailroom guy on an episode of *St. Elsewhere*, had a guest-starring role as a rich, philandering bachelor attacked by a rabid dog in an episode of a Fox show called *Likely Suspects*, and played a cameraman in *Die Hard 2*. I also started to make some money doing commercials. I did more than seventy-five "takes" biting into a chicken and mushroom sandwich for a Jack in the Box commercial. In case you're curious, to make it look "camera ready," they spray the burger with half a can of PAM. To this day, I've never eaten another Jack in the Box sandwich.

Around 1987, I had an audition for a new horror movie. It was called *Evil Dead II*. Now I'd never even heard of *Evil Dead I*, nor was I familiar with the director, Sam Raimi. But this was the big screen! The cast was flown to Wadesboro, North Carolina, for filming (wow, man, check out the legroom in first class)! I sat for hours having special effects makeup applied and had an absolute blast shooting the movie. I made some darn good money too . . . and then proceeded to blow it all on a trip to Europe. Suze Orman would not have been happy with my long-term financial planning at the time. It was getting exciting.

But the truth is, for every role you get, there are many more you don't. I tested for one of the leads on *The Young and the Restless*. I'd done scenes on the show in the past, but this was big. To make things even more stressful, a CBS show called *48 Hours* was doing a special on soaps at the time of my audition. They brought a camera crew to my little place (quick, clean the bathroom)! They filmed everything, from going over lines, to knotting my tie, to nervously waiting to audition. It was like a precursor to reality TV. They even filmed the audition. The episode aired in prime time. When the executive producer, Bill Bell, said, "He's too young—maybe cast him for another part down the road," I knew it meant, "We've decided to go another way." Ouch, national television rejection. Little did I know that *not* getting the job would open up an entirely new career. A manager, David Rini, had seen the *48 Hours* segment, which was all ad lib. He called. "That was funny," he said. "Have you ever thought of hosting live television?"

◆ ◆ ◆ ◆

Right around this time, Amy and I were having late-night conversations. The spark was alive. She would describe aspects of the art history class she was taking, bad college food, and walking with friends to a party with a windchill of minus-ten degrees. I would describe palm trees, weather at seventy-two degrees and sunny, and the commercial I'd just gotten (well, almost gotten—most of the time I just reported getting a callback that I'd find out about the following week). Conversations led to letters (yes, snail-mail letters). The "maybe someday you can visit" conversation finally became a reality when she had her first do over: she took a little break from school and moved to L.A. We were together. Now what?

We were just a couple of midwestern, small-town folk livin' in the big city. We took trips exploring the Gaslamp Quarter of San Diego, the mountains at Big Bear, and the desert of Joshua Tree National Park. There was an unforgettable excursion up the California coast to Santa Barbara for my thirtieth birthday. I even got together with a musician friend, Ray, and wrote and recorded a love song for her twenty-second birthday. It was called "When I Met You." It was either a witty country parody or the corniest love song ever written. Not sure. Amy worked as a nanny, and for a while had a waitressing job in downtown L.A. During my bartending days, she would join me after her shift, and I would flirt with the prettiest girl at the bar. It was a great time and went on for three wonderful years.

It was about that time that we started having those talks. You know the talks. The talks you have when you're living in the moment but haven't really decided exactly what the future holds. The "yes, we're together," but "are we . . . *together?*" talks. Is this relationship moving forward? In five years, what does together mean? In the past, I could always fall back on the "I'm too young" excuse. But at thirty, well, not so much. Had we been living in the Land of Ten Thousand Lakes, we'd probably have gotten married soon, and I'd be happily ice fishing on Green Lake right now. But this was L.A. I'd always had some sort of bizarre preconceived notion in my mind of what a guy needs in order to get married and have a family. And kids? It seemed like such an abstract thought. But the truth is, if you wait until you're absolutely, positively ready and secure, will you ever be ready? Would anyone? I was still focused on my work, living in the moment, and keeping that discussion at arm's length. Everything was fine. Or, maybe not.

Within a period of about three weeks, my whole world came crashing down. Amy and I were attending the wedding of friends of ours. All was hunky-dory on my end, but I knew she was upset about something. Was it the food? My cologne? "I . . . don't . . . want to . . . do this . . . anymore," she said, and started to cry. This was definitely not about the food. This was about us. She was serious. Now I was crying. This was really happening. Because I was so hardheaded, seeing only from my own point of view, I hadn't been listening to what she'd been trying to tell me for a while. I never saw it coming and felt like an SUV had just crashed into the side of my Honda and demolished it. But this time, *I* was the Honda. The biggest kick in the head was that I realized, for the first time, I had just lost the love of my life.

Look, I know, I didn't have cancer and I wasn't dying, and people break up all the time. Man up. Get over it. But the fact is, I was a mess. I'd take long walks, which was a little crazy, because nobody walks in L.A. I even started listening to broken-hearted country songs on the radio. It was pathetic. Yep, it was that bad. The only time it helped was in acting class. If a scene required tears, I was there. In fact, even if it didn't require tears,

I was there. To make matters more interesting, my manager was quitting the business for health reasons. In the boxing match of life, this was the one-two punch that had me on the ropes. I was broke—and, in a city of 20 million people, very much alone.

◆ ◆ ◆ ◆

I felt like I was literally starting from scratch and determined that if I ever got the chance again, I wasn't going to blow it. All I could do was focus on the things I could influence. I started to focus on getting work. Instead of looking for another agent and waiting for that phone to finally ring, I started making the calls myself, in essence, acting as *my own* manager. "Look, you gotta see this guy!" I would say. It was like phone sales, except I was the product. I was bound and determined to book a steady job on television, come hell or high water. Lo and behold, it started to work. From the various hosting auditions I'd been on, I'd gotten roles in a few pilots. Though the shows had never seen the light of day, I now had a great "host reel" to show producers. Then one night, while channel surfing, I came across a new channel that had just been added to my cable system. It was QVC. Some woman named Kathy Levine was on. It was completely different from the other shopping channels. It was warm and friendly. And the host was genuinely funny. I said to myself, "You know what, I could do that." I found out the entire operation was a galaxy away, in West Chester, Pennsylvania, of all places. I called, sent the tape, pitched myself, and basically said, "Look, you gotta see this guy." They saw the tape and called back.

Flying to West Chester, getting the call back, and finally landing the QVC gig was life changing. But it also meant leaving
L.A. Though we weren't together, Amy and I met for coffee to
say our good-byes. Was the spark still there? If it was, it didn't
matter. She was seeing someone else. Ouch again. I was still a
basket case. This was going to be a real do over.

But the job at QVC was working. I fell in love with live TV
and the immediate response from viewers. I enjoyed working
with the inventors who brought the products and the entire
team who made this 24/7 machine happen. I also went through
some horrible, laughable dating moments. Bad chemistry, little
chemistry, no chemistry. One date went so far as to insult a certain celebrity at a corporate QVC Christmas party. She told her
she "appreciated" the fact that, as a woman, she'd "let herself
age" and "allowed her wrinkles to show." The celebrity sold anti-
aging skin-care products. There was no second date.

Summer was approaching. I wanted to go back to Minnesota,
see my parents and friends, and, oh yah, have a beer or two at
good ol' Heritagefest. While there, under the big tent, with
polka music blaring, I looked out of the corner of my eye. It was
Amy. She was with another guy. I couldn't even believe my own
reaction. I was frozen. I couldn't move. I was still in love.

When I returned to Pennsylvania, I chatted with Lisa, a friend
from high school. "It's not over between you two," she said. "I
know it." I decided to write to Amy, just to catch up. How's
your new life? Will you get married? Although I was lonely and
feeling sorry for myself, it turns out things weren't "perfect" for

her either. She was breaking up. We had a supersecret rendezvous in Minneapolis at a Vikings football game. I wasn't sure what the outcome of this game was going to be, but as the crowd cheered, I was cheering inside as well. Could this really be happening? Could we get a second chance?

After many late-night phone calls, a visit, and a long car ride to Pennsylvania, it happened. Amy and I got back together. That Christmas Eve, with laughter, joyful tears, and the '50s classic "Earth Angel" playing on the stereo, I got down on one knee.

All Together Now

Today, those abstract thoughts about children have miraculously manifested themselves into two amazing, very real people. Nick and Josh are becoming young men now, and our lives are filled with baseball practices, homework, football games, and yes, the million-and-one other things busy parents do. I still have this crazy job at QVC, and it's given me the opportunity to travel to some pretty amazing places and meet some pretty amazing people. And though we've lived in Pennsylvania for more than fifteen years, we still love returning to our small Minnesota town, our home where it all began.

Reflections

Some years back, I was having a long talk with my dad. He was eighty-five at the time and getting very forgetful. Okay, who am I kidding? He was dying. He had trouble remembering what he'd had for lunch earlier in the day. But when the conversation shifted to World War II, his memory seemed to shift as well. Like many of his contemporaries, he rarely spoke about the war and the horrors associated with it. As he told stories of his days in the navy, I was transfixed. The images were sharp and vivid. I felt like I was watching a movie. Suddenly, he was no longer my aging father. He was a tall, strong, twenty-two-year-old "gunner's mate first class" on the USS *Boise*. It was midnight, in the middle of the Pacific Ocean, and the *Boise* was being attacked by six Japanese warships. Within thirty-six terrifying minutes, eighty-eight men were killed, many of them friends of my father. Miraculously, my father survived. Moments like that one, and countless others, are a reminder of the sacrifices people have made for our country. He spoke of the extraordinary VJ Day celebration ending the war. He recalled the joy of marrying my mom, Phyllis (still beautiful at eighty-five, they were married for sixty-one happy years). As the "movie" ended, I looked over at him. I once again saw an eighty-five-year-old man. There was a long silence. He then asked a very simple, yet profound question of the ages: "Where did the time go?"

It's those kinds of moments when we all reflect on the lightning speed at which time passes. We're suddenly shocked at the reminder that we're not gettin' any younger, our days are numbered. It's also an opportunity to ask ourselves, "What the heck am I gonna do with the rest of my life?" When I'm eighty-five years old and watching the "movie of my life" in my own mind, what kind of movie will it be? Will it be an action/adventure flick? A romantic comedy? Will it have a happy ending?

"Time is the coin of your life," Carl Sandburg once said. "It's the only coin you have, and only you can determine how it will be spent."

The extraordinary people profiled in this book couldn't have been more varied. Each of them came from different backgrounds, were blessed with unique gifts, and faced challenges that were distinctly their own. But as Max and I delved deeper into their stories, a common theme did, in fact, emerge. At some point, at a pivotal moment in the movie of their life, they stopped the action and yelled "CUT"! They decided the scene wasn't working. In fact, they came to the conclusion that the script itself needed a major rewrite. With imagination, focus, and no shortage of blood, sweat, and tears, they created an entirely new story.

You've taken precious time to read this book. Our hope is that it inspired you to "take five" and look at your own story. If you love the way that story is playing out, bravo. But if, as writer, director, and star, you feel the need to "add more action," "change the ending," or "make it more of a love story," then these stories should serve as a glowing reminder that a new plot twist is entirely possible. Your break is now over. You're wanted on the set. Lights, Camera . . . Action!

Permissions

The Great Holtzie © Adam Holtz. Printed with permission.

Taking Life by Storm © René Uzé. Printed with permission.

Do Over or Die © George Stella. Printed with permission.

Sing My Life © Meghan Cary. Printed with permission.

100 Sounds to See © Marsha Engle. Printed with permission.

From Disappointment to Reappointment © Tessa Simmons. Printed with permission.

Shoulder to Shoulder with Success © Kathleen Kirkwood. Printed with permission.

Victories © Peggy Fleming. Printed with permission.

One Act of Courage, a Whole New Life Path © Jim Eschrich. Printed with permission.

Those Two Boys © Michael Trufant. Printed with permission.

A Reinvention to Quack About © Jeanne Bice. Printed with permission.

Transformation © Shannon Hammer. Printed with permission.

Full Circle © Larry Koenig, Ph.D. Printed with permission.

A Little Contour, a Lot of Courage © Laura Geller. Printed with permission.

Three Feet from the Ditch © John Manda. Printed with permission.

About the Authors

As a senior program host on QVC, viewers across America have been inviting television host **Rick Domeier** into their homes for more than sixteen years. *Business 2.0 Magazine* described him as "A whirlwind of energy in the studio," and CNBC's *The Big Idea with Donnie Deutsch* described him as "The hardest working guy on television."

Through his hosting at QVC, one of the world's leading multi-channel lifestyle networking, he has had the opportunity to interview countless celebrities and entrepreneurs, from Heidi Klum to Suze Orman to Quincy Jones to Michael Dell of Dell Computers. He travels the world to help bring his audiences some of the newest and most unique products available. QVC is seen in 100 million homes and delivers more than 100 million packages a year. He has been also seen on every major broadcast network and has been called upon to do a variety of marketing projects for QVC, including overlooking New Yorkers on the Jumbotron in Times Square and appearing in an episode of *Celebrity Apprentice*. As a creative producer, Rick has enjoyed much success producing and hosting in QVC favorites like *tech*CONNECT *w. Rick, Rick & Easy Cooking,* and as a certified personal trainer and fitness fanatic, *Get Fit w. Rick.* He created and produced the first online "Shop Opera," a hilarious soap opera spoof starring Joan Rivers. Domeier has won a number of awards for his efforts, including the Ace Award, the Gem Award, two Q-Emmys, and the Cornerstone Award—QVC's highest honor. He is also a public speaker and classically trained actor. From the Shakespearean stage to the big and small screen, his television and movie credits include *Die Hard II, The Young and the Restless,* and a costarring role in the unforgettable Sam Raimi cult classic *Evil Dead II.* A theatre major, Domeier is a scholarship recipient and graduate of the Drama School at SCR. Despite his successful career, what matters most to Rick is being a husband and father. He spends his free time with his wife and two sons and volunteers in his community. A YMCA supporter, Rick is a proud "chief" of his Adventure Guides and a coach for his sons' baseball and football teams, the Marsh Creek Eagles. He also supports his local chapter of Habitat for Humanity and contributes to the American Diabetes Association.

A "pathological optimist," Domeier is currently reinventing himself. *Can I Get A Do Over?* is his first book.

Max Davis holds degrees in journalism and theology. He is the author of sixteen books and has been featured on *The Today Show, USA Today*, and *The 700 Club*. In addition to his own works, Max has done numerous collaboration and ghostwriting projects. He is also a sought-after speaker and media personality. Visit him at www.MaxDavisbooks.com.

Visit www.canigetadoover.com.